# VISIONARIES, BUILDERS, & MAINTAINERS

*The People You Need to Make Change Succeed*

## KENNETH E. FIELDS

### TEAM FIELDS PUBLISHING

For information:
teamfieldspublishing.com

ISBN: 0988436205
ISBN-13: 9780988436206

*To Kenton and Kade*

*"Twenty years from now you will be more
disappointed by the things [that] you didn't do
than by the ones [that] you did do. So throw off the
bowlines. Sail away from the safe harbour.
Catch the trade winds in your sails.
Explore. Dream. Discover."*

— attributed to Mark Twain

# Acknowledgements

I would like to thank:

Miles Terry, who helped me formalize the main idea during a late-night conversation outside a Home Depot in Greenville, SC.

Jeff White, who never stopped asking 'How's the book going?'

Danny Branyon, who kept the dream alive during several conversations at the Bui-Bui in Clermont-Ferrand, France.

Johannes Mutzke for his insight, support, and invaluable feedback.

Peter Ramirez and Melody Mosley for their comments on the initial manuscript.

My dad, Jim Fields. Here's my first book, now it's your turn. Every year since 1996 has been a gift. Thanks, Gayle, for taking such good care of him.

My mom, Gwin St. John, for making me run home after I wanted to quit the 6th grade track team. Anything important enough to start is important enough to finish.

Bob and Judy Galbert for opening your family to me and raising such a wonderful daughter.

My smart, funny, and beautiful (inside and out) wife, Kelly Fields, who always believed I could do this. You are a wonderful mother and supportive wife. I am blessed to have you in my life.

# Table of Contents

Acknowledgements . . . . . . . . . . . . . . . . . . . . . . . v

Table of Contents . . . . . . . . . . . . . . . . . . . . . . . vii

Prologue . . . . . . . . . . . . . . . . . . . . . . . . . . . . .ix

A Parable . . . . . . . . . . . . . . . . . . . . . . . . . 1-103

Epilogue . . . . . . . . . . . . . . . . . . . . . . . . . .119

So, now what? . . . . . . . . . . . . . . . . . . . . . . .123

Visionaries . . . . . . . . . . . . . . . . . . . . . . . . .127

Builders . . . . . . . . . . . . . . . . . . . . . . . . . . .133

Maintainers . . . . . . . . . . . . . . . . . . . . . . . . .139

Conclusion . . . . . . . . . . . . . . . . . . . . . . . . .145

Appendix 1 . . . . . . . . . . . . . . . . . . . . . . . . 149

Notes . . . . . . . . . . . . . . . . . . . . . . . . . . . . .151

# Prologue

It was time. The owner of the old home at 816 W. Main Street had decided to paint his son's room. The old home had seen its share of white walls but T.J. and his wife, Jill, wanted something different for their first child, due in February. After spending what seemed like hours (although it was just over twenty minutes) of their Saturday morning looking at colored pieces of paper, they had chosen Robin Egg Blue by MastersPaint. It matched the theme Jill had seen in one of the seemingly hundreds of baby magazines that were showing up at their door and, T.J. hoped, might subconsciously encourage his son to love the outdoors and the trees, and the birds and all those things that made his heart come alive.

T.J. and Jill had only been married a few years when they realized that having children might not be as easy for them as it was for other couples. Through numerous doctors and treatments, they had almost given up hope until seven months ago, when Jill mentioned that she might be pregnant. One plus sign affirmation later, they were excited and in shock and in love with a little one that was targeted to arrive on February 8, Jill's late grandfather's birthday.

And that brings us back to the empty, white room that would soon become a crossroads of poopy diapers, spit up cloths, stuffed ducks, tiny clothes, and late night rocking sessions. Plain, flat, white just wouldn't do. So, with the can of Robin Egg Blue in hand, T.J. walked to the painting supplies while Jill went to check out the closet organizers.

McKinney Hardware had been supplying do-it-yourselfers and do-it-for-otherers for over eighty years and T.J. could remember walking its well supplied aisles as a child with his father. He quickly arrived at the painting supplies and methodically began running his eyes over each shelf. T.J. was a little surprised at the number of choices. There were rollers in blue, pink, and cream with a nap from 3/16" to 3/8". Angled and straight brushes sized between one and three inches. Finally, he saw foam brushes from one to four inches. Choices, choices, choices.

Since he was only painting one room, T.J. was sure that all he needed was a couple of rollers and a 'roller frame.' He scanned the rollers and decided on a three-pack of 3/8" rollers from Vision—"The big name in paint." The blue-and-white package offered "maximum coverage" and the promise, "The only roller you'll need!" That sounded good, because with the baby on the way, T.J. and Jill were on a budget. That choice made, T.J. decided on a roll of blue painter's tape, a roller tray and frame combo, and a plastic drop cloth.

He was carrying his choices toward the closet supplies when Jill rounded the corner. "Find anything?" he asked.

"I don't know, honey," she said. "There are a lot of choices, but I just didn't see what I was looking for."

T.J. put his arm around her and gave her a squeeze. "We have a couple more months, we'll keep looking." They turned to head toward the front of the store when T.J. caught a glimpse of McKinney

Hardware's current owner, Reid McKinney. He was easily recognizable by his shock of white hair. After running the store for almost sixty years, Reid's father, Richard, had turned the store over to Reid more than twenty years ago. T.J. had known Reid most of his life, beginning when Reid coached his Little League team, the Rotary Reds.

As T.J. put his paint rollers and other supplies on the worn counter, Reid caught his eye and smiled. "How's it goin' there, T.J.?" he asked.

"Fine, sir," T.J. replied.

"And, Jill, how are you feeling? You keepin' this boy straight?"

Jill smiled. "Doin' the best I can, Mr. McKinney."

"Call me Reid...Mr. McKinney hasn't been a regular here for years! It looks like you two are getting ready to paint something...maybe that new baby's room? What is it about new mamas and nesting? I remember when me and Martha were getting ready for our first one. Seems like she organized the whole house! She alphabetized the pantry, the bookshelf, you name it. Anyway, let's see what you have here. Paint, rollers, drop cloth..." As Reid said each item, he put the price into the ancient cash register from memory. He'd never seen the need to go to one of those fancy bar code scanners, and besides, it gave him the opportunity to lower the price of his merchandise a dollar or two when he thought folks needed the help. As he entered the price for the last items and placed them in a plain, brown paper bag, a puzzled look crossed his face.

"So, T.J., do you have any brushes at home?" Reid asked.

"Nope," said T.J., "this is the first time we've ever painted anything so we came here to get all of our supplies."

Reid smiled a knowing smile. "Well, we sure do appreciate your business. I guess we'll be seeing you back here real soon."

T.J. put his right hand out to shake Reid's and crumpled the top of the paper bag as he grabbed it with his left. "See you later, Mr. McKinney!" T.J. said as he and Jill walked out the door.

As T.J. and Jill drove home, they were lost in their own thoughts. She was visualizing the baby's room, with its cheery blue walls and white furniture. Jill imagined a cute jungle scene on the wall and, of course, a cooing baby in the crib, smiling at its mother. T.J. couldn't get his mind off of some issues he recently had at work. He had joined Lackey & Durham, a local manufacturer, just over five years ago and been a crew manager for the past two. T.J.

felt sure that Andy, his old boss, was the best shop manager anyone could ever hope to work for. However, he had recently gotten a new boss who was not as easy to work with. That thought was interrupted as Jill screamed.

# Chapter One

*L**ay off the horn, man, we're all stuck at the light here!* T.J. thought. The sound was so loud that it seemed like it was inside his head. Then he heard a soft groan beside him. Jill! T.J. shook his head and opened his eyes. Jill was still beside him, looking at him, her eyes wide with fear. She was holding her stomach. "Are you OK?" T. J. asked.

She nodded her head. "I think I just went into labor!"

That brought T.J. into full consciousness. He pulled himself off the steering wheel and the car horn stopped. Then, exiting the driver's side, he tried to walk around the front of the car. As he did, he found the reason for Jill's initial scream. A green Dodge from the 1960s had ignored the traffic light now directly above it. The driver was a small, white-haired force of nature, walking in circles while waving her hands. Jill wouldn't be getting out of the car the same way she got in.

As T.J. ran back to his door, a police officer arrived.

"Anyone hurt?" she asked.

"My wife is seven months pregnant and she just went into labor!" T.J. shouted as he opened the driver's side door to help Jill out of the car. Shaken, Jill climbed across the center console and into the driver's side before turning to face the officer. She suddenly moved her hands to her stomach and groaned.

"Let's get you to the hospital now," the officer said. "My name is Officer Bishop. Why don't you and your husband get in the back of my squad car and I'll take you."

As the police cruiser sped toward Memorial Hospital, Jill squeezed T.J.'s hand tightly every ninety seconds. Officer Bishop was on the radio communicating the situation to the hospital. When she pulled the car into the covered entrance marked EMER-GENCY in large white letters on a red sign, a nurse was waiting with a wheelchair. The nurse opened Jill's door and helped her into the chair. She gave a tight smile to T.J. as she said, "Thanks, Officer, we've got it from here." T.J. was coming around the back of the car to follow Jill as Officer Bishop said, "Sir, I know you want to be with your wife but I do need to ask you a few questions about the accident." T.J. was surprised at first but decided that he would have to do this sooner or later and called out to Jill, "I'll be with you as quickly as I can. I love you!"

The officer was efficient and had taken an official statement from T.J. in less than ten minutes. She thanked him for his cooperation and prepared to join her colleagues still at the scene of the accident. She assured T.J. that he had nothing to worry about and reminded him to call his insurance agent. He decided to make that call as he headed inside. After explaining the situation to Harold, the insurance agent his parents had known for more than thirty years, he almost ran to the admission desk to find out about Jill. The same nurse that had wheeled Jill into the hospital met him at the desk. "Mr. Hughes," she said, "my name is Sarah, I'm a nurse here and I can take you to your wife now." T.J. was so thankful that he almost hugged her.

He followed the nurse down the hall. She stopped in front of a door with a 'wood-grained' plastic plate reading *105*. "Your wife's in here. We've given her some drugs to slow the contractions, so she may seem a little woozy. I'll send the doctor by to give you an update. T.J. hesitated as he opened the door. They had waited so long for this baby. Would he even get to meet his son? Was his wife OK? All of these questions seemed safe as they were unanswered on this side of the door, but after he opened it, his life might never be the same again. He whispered a prayer as he twisted the knob and took a step into the dimly lit room.

# Chapter Two

"Jill," he whispered. He took another step into the room, and as his eyes adjusted, he realized that in a few short minutes, his wife had gone from expectant mother to high-risk hospital patient. She opened her eyes as he closed the door behind him. "Hey," she said as she smiled weakly.

He put his hand up to her face. "Hey," he said. "How's it going? It looks like you've got a lot going on." Suddenly, T.J. was aware of a repetitive sound that reminded him of a horse galloping. What was that? "Jill," he asked, "what's that sound? Is it your heart?"

"No," Jill replied, as a tear ran down her cheek. "It's the baby's."

They listened in silence for what seemed like thirty minutes, in awe of this unique connection with their child. T.J. sat down beside the bed and took Jill's hand. As he did, he noticed something hard on the back of her hand. There was an IV bag connected to her via a tube. "What's this?" he said. "Magnesium something or the other," Jill replied. "The doctor said that it will slow down the contractions but may make me feel a little funny until they stop giving it to me." "Are you OK?" she asked. Honestly, T.J. hadn't taken the time to think about how he was doing. He stood up, stretched, and sat back down. "I'll be a little sore tomorrow but everything seems to be working. Is there anything you need?" "No," Jill replied, "but I am going to close my eyes for a minute. One of the medicines they gave me made me a little sleepy." T.J. stayed in the room, rubbing Jill's hand and listening to the amazing heartbeat of his son until Jill was asleep. He quietly stood up, pulled the curtains to darken the room, and walked back into the hallway to look for someone who could tell him when Jill could go home.

As he took a right into the hallway, T.J. almost ran into someone.

"Mr. Hughes?" the person asked.

"Yes," T.J. replied.

"My name is Dr. Chittick; I think that you met my wife, Sarah, as you came in. Why don't we walk outside for a minute?" As they walked, the doctor continued, "As a result of the accident, your wife went into premature labor. The contractions were strong but we seem to have them under control. We're giving her magnesium sulfate and will continue to do so for the next twenty-four hours. We'll then keep her under observation another twenty-four hours to be sure that the contractions have stopped. Based on what we see, she may have to take medication as a precaution for the rest of the pregnancy, but I am not concerned that the baby will be delivered pre-term." T.J. breathed a sigh of relief. Dr. Chittick continued, "I'm sure that you and your wife are very scared right now so please feel free to ask any questions." Wife OK, check. Baby OK, check. No, T.J. didn't have any questions right now. He thanked the doctor and headed back to his wife's room. Dr. Chittick's wife, the nurse, was there, checking Jill's heart rate.

"Mr. Hughes," she said, "your wife will be asleep for a few hours, so you're welcome to head home to rest a little yourself. She should be awake later this afternoon."

T.J. decided that putting his brain in neutral might be a good idea so he thanked the nurse and headed for his car. On the way to the front door, he remembered that he had left his car in the middle of the road when the officer had taken them to the hospital. How was he going to get it back? Lost in thought, he was startled when another nurse at the front desk called his name. "T.J. Hughes?" she asked. His startled look answered her question. "Officer Bishop left this card for you. She said you could claim the belongings from your car here." T.J. looked at the business card she gave him. In simple black text it read: COUNTY POLICE IMPOUND LOT, 2995 STANLEY VALLEY ROAD, (555) 272-3442. He thanked the nurse and headed out into the late morning sunshine.

# Chapter Three

As noon approached, T.J. and his friend Shawn pulled into the impound lot, the gravel crunching under the tires. The officer on duty recognized Shawn's car and came out to open the eight-foot-tall chain-link gate. "Heard about the wreck, T.J.," Deputy Biggs said. "How ya feelin'?"

"Not bad," replied T.J. "Jill's going to be in the hospital for a few days. I'm heading back as soon as I clean out the car. We left a few things in there."

"I can understand you were in a hurry," said the deputy. "The tow truck just brought your car in... it's at the end of the first row."

Shawn walked into the heated main building with Deputy Biggs, a friend since kindergarten. "How's he doin'?" the deputy asked.

"Not bad, Jason," Shawn replied. "He's still a little shocked by how quick it happened."

"Yeah," Jason replied, "one minute you're hanging out with your wife on a Saturday, the next minute you're, well, here, looking at your wrecked car."

"How bad was the car?" Shawn asked.

"It didn't look bad to me but we see all kinds here. I've learned that there's not much of a relationship between how bad the car looks and how bad the folks involved were injured."

As his friends were talking about the condition of his car, T.J. was assessing it first-hand. The right front quarter panel was significantly damaged . Some green paint was visible near the bumper. The tire seemed to be in good shape, although it too had some scuffs. Who knew what the insurance agent would say. T.J. sighed as he walked toward the passenger door. He put his hand on the handle and pulled. Nothing. His eyes followed the outline of the door to the gap in the door and the front quarter panel. He could see a large dent where the sheet metal was bent, causing the door not to open. How wide was that lady's car anyway? T.J. gave the door one last pull. No luck. He walked around the back of the car to the driver's side door, which opened normally. He pulled all of the insurance and ownership papers out of the glove compartment. Buried under them he found a pen, a tire pressure gage…just some odds and ends. He looked around where Jill was sitting. From inside the car, it all looked normal. Jill's hot chocolate from their earlier visit to the Donut Hole was now cold. He pulled it out of the console and set it on top of the car to take with him. Nothing else stood out in the front. He had just cleaned the car, so the back and trunk were empty. He turned to go and remembered Jill's cold hot chocolate on the roof of the car.

As he turned around, something brown in the back seat caught his eye. It was the paper bag of painting supplies from McKinney's. That little shopping trip seemed like an eternity ago. He opened the rear driver's side door and dropped all of the miscellaneous stuff he had collected from the car into the bag. He picked up the bag and the paint and placed them on the ground. As he shut the door, he instinctively reached for his keys to lock the car. He laughed at himself…no need to lock an empty car that no one could drive sitting behind an eight-foot fence and guarded by a sheriff's deputy, right? He smiled, bent over to pick up the bag and the paint, and, overcome by the emotion of the morning, started to cry.

# Chapter Four

W hile loading the items from T.J.'s car into Shawn's truck, the tearstains on T.J.'s face were evident. Shawn wasn't comfortable around anyone crying, especially someone he had known since first grade. "So how's work going?" Shawn asked.

The question briefly sent T.J. into a déjà vu state. He had been thinking about work when the accident happened. He shook his head to get rid of the sensation. "Well, Hoyt, my new boss, is as different as night from day compared to Andy," T.J. began, thankful for the opportunity to think about anything other than what was going on in the hospital. "Andy was always thinking about the big picture, how all of the pieces fit together to keep Lackey & Durham relevant." The fifty-year-old company was one of the major employers in the town, and Andy had recently been promoted to a position on the plant staff. "Hoyt could pick a gnat off a log at two hundred yards, as Grandpa Jim used to say. He seems more interested in making sure the shop floor is clean and the pliers are in the right place than he is in the improvements that will keep us around another fifty years."

"Well, he's only been in his job for a few weeks," said Shawn, "it's bound to get better." T.J. wasn't so sure.

As they pulled into T.J. and Jill's driveway, T.J. sighed loudly. Jill's car was right where it should be and the columned porch where they both loved to sit in the swing hadn't moved. At least some things were stable. He thanked Shawn for his help and time as he exited the car. His foot brushed the bag. He felt kind of silly carrying painting stuff into the house as his wife lay in the hospital. He turned as he headed for the back door and waved at Shawn. Shawn smiled back as he began to turn his car around. T.J. put the can of paint and the bag down on the porch and pulled the keys out of his pocket. He unlocked the door and entered the empty house that seemed quieter today. After turning around to watch Shawn leave the driveway, he picked up the paint, rollers, and other supplies and dropped them off in the baby's room.

A quick shower and change of clothes later, he was packing a bag to take to Jill at the hospital. He had only been gone for two hours but it seemed like forever. He walked outside to get in Jill's car, an old Honda Accord she had been driving since they met in college. On the drive to the hospital, he was extra watchful at every intersection. One accident today was enough. He laughed at himself when he noticed he was sitting on the edge of his seat, just like Jill's dad, Eric. He stopped in mid-laugh as he remembered that he still hadn't talked to anyone in the family. He would have to make some calls as soon as he got to the hospital—which he had just passed on the left. He took a right at the light into the parking lot at Charlie's, his favorite barbeque place, and turned around in the parking lot. The light was red by the time he turned around, so he waited impatiently. The light changed, and although he normally would have floored it as soon as that happened, the morning's experiences made him hesitate. "Holy cow!" T.J. said, as a blue convertible raced through the intersection. He took a nice, slow left back onto Highway 66 and a gentle right into the hospital parking lot. That might be enough driving for a while.

# Chapter Five

T.J. had only been away from room 105 for a few hours, but as he opened the door, it was evident that the room's sole resident was feeling better. The curtains were open, letting the late afternoon sunlight stream in. Jill was sitting up in the bed talking to Nurse Sarah as the nurse repositioned the discs being used to monitor the baby's heartbeat. Jill smiled as she noticed T.J. enter the room and she patiently waited for the nurse to finish her work.

"That'll do," said Sarah. "Mr. Hughes, your wife and baby are doing quite well. We're still monitoring the baby's heartbeat, but he seems to be a trooper." T.J. gave her the 'yeah, my kid is tough' new dad look. Sarah continued, "The magnesium sulfate is going to make it tough for your wife's eyes to focus on anything for a while, and she'll feel flushed and warm until we take her off it. The good news is that should be tomorrow. I'll be back to check on you at five thirty. Mrs. Hughes, dinner will be roast pork with mashed potatoes. It's the chef's specialty...hope you're hungry!"

"Blech," Jill said as the door shut. "Who can think about eating at a time like this?" Actually, T.J. could. He just realized he hadn't eaten anything since breakfast, but he figured now wasn't the best time to have that discussion.

"How's it going?" T.J. asked as he bent down to kiss his wife's damp face. "Not great. I feel miserable; I can't even watch TV because of my eyes. Our little buddy just loves the fact that I'm laying down in the middle of the day. He's watching a workout video or something in there!" She paused. "But then I listen to that little heart and I forget about all of that stuff. I'm so happy he's alive that the rest of the problems seem kind of small." Thankful tears welled up in her eyes as she reached for T.J.'s hand. "So, how are you feeling?" The be-dup, be-dup, be-dup of his son's heartbeat filled in every gap in the conversation.

"Can we turn the volume down on junior?" T.J. asked. "He's a little noisy."

"He's keeping me company," Jill said. "So, unless you're spending the night in that chair, let's leave him be."

T.J. and Jill called each of their parents to let them know what was going on. Then they talked for a few minutes about the eventful morning. Jill tried valiantly to stay in the conversation but after fifteen minutes, she closed her eyes and let her head roll to the center of the pillow.

"Ready for a nap?" asked T.J.

"I think so," she said as she pulled up the covers. "Visiting hours end at six. Why don't you head home and come see me in the morning?"

T.J. sat beside her, watching her breathe and listening to that little heartbeat for what seemed like hours. He was so grateful for the opportunity to be with his family that he didn't want to leave. He laid his head over to the side of the chair, closed his eyes, and soon, all three of them were sound asleep.

# Chapter Six

When T.J. woke up, he noticed that Jill's dinner had been delivered and the large clock on the wall said it was 7:15 p.m. T.J. shook some of the cobwebs out of his head and stood up. Jill was still sound asleep, so he kissed her on the forehead as she turned her head on the pillow. As he reached for the door, he became conscious of the be-dup of that little heart. He blew the baby a kiss as he closed the door and headed for the parking lot.

On his short drive home, he pondered what he could do alone at home to stay busy on a Saturday evening. It was that painful time in December after the final regular season college games but before the bowls started, so he would have to wait for tomorrow for his football fix. T.J. rolled into the driveway and parked the car. He had to admit that coming home seemed pretty lonely knowing Jill wouldn't be there. As he walked through the kitchen, he realized how little he had eaten today. He made a sandwich, grabbed a bag of chips, and headed for the TV in the living room. He dined to the familiar sounds of *Jeopardy!* after a quick survey of the channels. As he returned to the kitchen with his empty plate, he looked into the baby's room and noticed the painting supplies on the floor. He thought that having the room painted would be a nice surprise for Jill when she got home and he was honestly excited about having something to do.

After a change of clothes, he opened the paper bag and laid out the contents on the floor. "OK, drop cloth first," he said to himself. The hardwood floors were several decades old and he was hoping to keep them in place for a couple of decades more. He opened the blue painter's tape and decided to tape off one wall. He started with the floorboard and then realized he was going to need some help to get tape up to the crown molding. He made his way to the outbuilding, unlocked the padlock, and pulled the stepladder off the wall. Heading back toward the house, he took a minute to look up. It was a clear, winter night and the stars were out in all their glory. He looked to the east, toward downtown, and quickly found the three stars in the belt of Orion. As he looked across the street, he saw the familiar shapes of the Big and Little Dippers. Those groups of stars had been 'friends' since his father pointed them out to him as a child. It was a nice night to have a few friends around.

Once inside with the ladder, he taped off the crown molding, which, by its appearance, was as old as the house. T.J. looked around the perimeter of the wall and decided it was time to open the paint. He shook it well and opened it; Robin Egg Blue, just the right color for a bouncing baby boy. As he poured the paint into the tray, he was tempted to put his finger in it and have a taste. It looked smooth and sweet, like icing. Just then, the scent reached his nose and it definitely didn't smell like icing. He opened the rollers and the roller frame, put them together, and placed the roller in the paint. The cream-colored roller quickly soaked up the blue paint and he was ready for the first stroke. He was almost scared, like there was no turning back once the paint was on the wall. He positioned the roller in the middle of the wall, closed his eyes, and made the first stroke.

# Chapter Seven

T.J. painted the middle of the wall for twenty minutes and then got to the edges. With the roller, he was able to paint up to the tape on the bottom of the wall, but as he got to the corner and top of the wall, he realized that the roller was too big to get paint on the wall without getting it on the ceiling too. He placed the roller back in the pan and sat down on the floor. T.J. tilted his head and stared at the wall as if a giant hand was going to emerge and either paint the wall for him, or write out detailed painting instructions. After five minutes, neither happened and he decided that he needed help. As he got up, he noticed the other two rollers in the package from Vision. He couldn't argue with their claim of "maximum coverage." The middle of the wall looked pretty good. But, the promise "The only roller you'll need!" mocked him. Maybe he needed more than a roller. Mr. McKinney would know but the store was closed now and wouldn't be open on Sunday. Maybe he could run by on Monday after work to ask. He was pleased with the progress that he had made and decided to clean up. Tomorrow would be here before he knew it.

Sunday flew by. First, he drove downtown to attend the little storefront church that his family had been attending for years. He called Jill after church to learn that the doctor had taken her off most of the medications and her appetite had returned. So his next stop was Charlie's across the street from the hospital. He ordered two pulled pork plates with baked beans and coleslaw. As he walked into Jill's room, the scent of the food filled the small space. "Yum," Jill said, "that smells delicious!" She had slept until eight o'clock in the morning, when they stopped giving her the contraction-halting magnesium sulfate. "I had a couple of pieces of cinnamon toast this morning but the medication still made me a little sick to my stomach," she said.

"But this is real food! Let's eat." During their peaceful lunch on paper plates, they tried to figure out what the week ahead would look like. Jill should be ready to go home late Tuesday or early Wednesday morning so they agreed that T.J. would work Monday and Tuesday and stay home with her on Wednesday.

After lunch, Jill took a few minutes to call Dave Nash, her boss at Hamilton Bank. News of the accident had traveled quickly and Dave was glad to hear she was OK. He assured her that she could take all the time she needed to recover. As she got off the phone with Dave, Jill noticed T.J. staring out the window. "What's wrong?" she asked.

"I was just thinking...Dave has been such a great boss. He has really supported you during the pregnancy and cares about the people that work for him. Andy was like that…" T.J.'s voice trailed off. Jill knew what was coming next. Ever since Andy had been replaced by Hoyt, T.J. had been miserable at work. He and Andy had really seemed to complement each other. Andy's ability to see the big picture was balanced by T.J.'s ability to construct a realistic plan to make that picture a reality. Hoyt was definitely *not* a big picture kind of guy. Poor Jill had heard all about it for the past four months.

Jill sympathetically placed a hand on T.J.'s knee and settled in to listen to her frustrated husband. She was saved from another retelling of the story by Nurse Chittick. "Time for a blood pressure check!" she said cheerily.

"I'm guessing that you'll be checking some other stuff too," Jill muttered. "Should I leave you two alone?" asked T.J. "Well," said Jill, "I think I'll be ready for a nap when this fun is over. Lori called and said that she would stop here for supper." Lori and Jill had been best friends since they were neighbors at T.J. and Jill's first apartment. "Why don't you head home and give me a call around eight tonight?" It didn't hurt T.J.'s feelings to miss out on whatever the nurse would be checking and a Sunday afternoon of pro football would be a nice, relaxing diversion.

"OK, sweetie," he said. "I'll give you a call tonight. I love you." He bent down to give her a kiss and was happy to get a hug in return. Things were getting back to normal.

# Chapter Eight

The alarm clock buzzed loudly at T.J. He sat up and hit two or three things on the nightstand before the buzzing stopped. The red numbers read *6:05*. He felt ready for a new week. The baby emergency was almost over. On Sunday evening, Jill had been told that she would be coming home on Wednesday, so that was good news. No, it was actually great news. He had gotten a good night's sleep. He had a relaxing Sunday in front of the TV watching the games. So what was that nagging feeling in the back of his head?

Forty-five minutes later, the source of the fear or stress or whatever you wanted to call it was apparent. It had peaked when he pulled into the parking lot at Lackey & Durham. In the past, he could remember driving up to the brick plant and feeling a sense of pride and excitement. Lately it seemed that he dreaded the frustration each new day would bring. He spent five minutes in the parking lot listening to the radio before taking a deep breath and opening the car door. T.J. had never been the most talkative guy at work and he was thankful that he didn't see anyone he 'had' to talk to on the way in.

As he arrived at his desk, he was surprised to see the red message light on his phone illuminated. T.J.'s crew didn't work this weekend so he hadn't expected any news. He tapped in his voicemail number and password. *Four messages?* he thought. "T.J., this is Andy. Heard about Jill's accident and just wanted to let you know that my family and I are keeping you in our prayers." T.J. smiled. Classic Andy. Two other colleagues, Steve and Bob, had left him messages about Jill. They both offered to cover for him if he needed to be out. He made a note to run by their desks today and thank them. "Message four," the voicemail lady said, "from an outside number at six fifty-nine a.m." His brow crinkled as he tried to guess who it might be...he had just missed the call. "Hi, honey, it's me," Jill said, "Just wanted to let you know that the baby and I are doing fine this morning and we're thinking about you. Have a great day at work and we'll see you tonight. We love you!" He smiled. That was a good way to start the day.

After five minutes in his office making a plan for the day, T.J. headed out for the shop floor. As a crew manager, he was responsible for meeting the daily target handed down from the Planning department. Someone from Planning was responsible for posting the targets and the results for the last seven days every morning and the indicator board in his shop was his first stop every day. He already knew that last week's numbers were below target, so he wasn't surprised to see the 'yellow light' symbol beside the production indicator. He was surprised to see that this week's targets didn't seem to take into account the machine outage from last week, which caused his team to be below target. The problem was intermittent at the start of the week, but by Thursday, the TR1 was completely down and Maintenance was having a hard time finding the problem. It seemed the least Planning could do is project a decrease in output until Maintenance fixed the issue. He shook his head. Regardless of what he thought, T.J. didn't control Maintenance or Planning. He would have to elevate this problem.

As he visited his team, he was reminded what he enjoyed about his job. Most of the employees at Lackey & Durham had lived in the area all of their lives and they always had entertaining stories about their families, immediate and extended, after the weekend. He could never ask them, of course, but it seemed that they enjoyed working with him too. Often on Monday nights, he would bring home fresh vegetables or meat, depending on the season, that one of his crewmembers had brought him. A couple of people stopped him to ask about Jill. News travels fast in a small town, but T.J. was nevertheless surprised by how many people knew the story and how much they cared. As he made his way across the shop floor toward Hoyt's office, he noticed with surprise that Hoyt's door was shut and the lights weren't on. *Hmmmm,* he thought to himself, *that's strange. Hoyt is on time for everything!* In fact, it seemed like he had an internal clock that regulated his day. T.J. left a note on Hoyt's door: LOOKING FOR YOU. –T.J. Then he headed back toward his office.

# Chapter Nine

Hoyt dropped by to see T.J. around ten o'clock. "Saw your note on the door," said Hoyt. "What are you doing here? Your family needs you more than we do!" T.J. explained the plan for the week that he and Jill had made. "I'll only be here today and tomorrow. Jill's coming home on Wednesday and we'll play it by ear after that." "Fair enough, so what's up?" T.J. explained the issue with the TR1 and his frustrations with Maintenance and Planning. Hoyt listened and there was silence in the room for what seemed like five minutes after T.J. finished.

Finally, Hoyt spoke. "Sounds like a good issue for Friday's Shop Staff meeting." T.J. felt the hairs on his neck tingle and his shoulders become tense.

"Our production numbers from last week are off target and if we don't get this resolved, we're going to have the same problem this week." Didn't Hoyt understand this was urgent?

"I understand," Hoyt said, "but the other managers in the plant have their priorities too. Why don't we let them follow their standard processes and maybe this issue will go away by Friday?"

T.J. wanted to scream, "That's too late! We'll be so far behind that we'll never catch up for the month!" He restrained himself. He had tried that before with Hoyt and failed. It seemed that conflict agitated Hoyt instead of spurring him to action. He was sure that Andy would have proposed three solutions while he was explaining the problem and they would be on their way to talk to someone right now. But that wasn't Hoyt's way. He believed in following the standard process steps the same way every time. Any deviation from that was a problem...even if that deviation fixed a problem! T.J. stared at the floor and took a deep breath. "Friday's late, Hoyt. What do you say I give you an update before I leave on Tuesday night and you can push the issue on Wednesday if we still have it?"

"Fair enough," Hoyt replied.

T.J. spent the rest of the day listening to his team complain about the TR1 issue, accepting prayers and well wishes from everyone he saw, and wishing Andy were around to point him in the right direction on this problem. He closed his door at the end of the day, ready to see Jill. As he arrived at the car, he was reminded of another problem that needed help. The remaining Vision rollers were on the front seat in their package. He would make a quick stop at McKinney's before heading to the hospital.

# Chapter Ten

T.J. opened the wooden door at McKinney's and a little metal bell above it announced his arrival. "T.J.," said Mr. McKinney, as he smiled, "shouldn't you be at the hospital? We heard about Jill's accident. Sounds like it was right after y'all left here. How's she doin'?"

"We had a scare on Saturday but the doctors tell me that she's out of the woods. She'll be coming home on Wednesday."

"Fine news," said Mr. McKinney. "We prayed for her on Sunday. I'll talk to Martha about having the church ladies bring a meal over to you on

Wednesday. That'll give you something to eat until Jill can get back on her feet." The thought of food made T.J.'s stomach emit a low rumble. The folks at McKinney's Chapel (named for Mr. McKinney's grandfather who donated the land over a hundred years ago) were famous for their covered dish dinners. T.J. could only imagine what and who might show up at his house on Wednesday.

"That's very kind, sir. We'll just be happy to have her home. Please tell Mrs. McKinney not to go all out on account of us." T.J. smiled as he said it. Martha McKinney only knew one way to do things and that was with all of her heart. "Well, T.J.," Mr. McKinney sighed, "you know Martha. She just loves that kind of thing. Now that we've settled that, what I can I do for you?"

T.J. walked to the counter and placed the rollers on it. "I have a question, Mr. McKinney. I'm trying to paint this room as a surprise for Jill before she gets home. I started last night with the rollers but there's no way to get in the corners without painting the ceiling blue too! This package seems a little misleading to me," he said while pointing to the quote on the remaining Vision rollers—"The only roller you'll need!"

"Misleading?" asked Mr. McKinney. "Well, I have been using Vision rollers for years and I haven't had any problems. But that doesn't mean that they are the only tool you need to paint a room! Come back here with me."

They walked back to the painting supplies section that T.J had last visited on Saturday. So much had happened since then that it seemed like eons ago. Mr. McKinney picked up an unopened pack of Vision rollers. "Now, T.J.," he said "rollers are great for covering lots of territory but they work best when someone creates a frame for them to work in." He picked up a two and a half-inch angled brush from the Builder's Best line with a cardboard wrap in red and white. "First, load up your brush with paint. Then, pull it parallel and about an inch above the edge you want to paint." Mr. McKinney demonstrated with a steady hand that seemed at odds with the thin, white hair that communicated his age. "That creates a reservoir for you to pull right up to the edge with a nice, clean line," he said as he finished painting the imaginary line with a flourish. "You use the brush to create a frame and then the roller to cover the inside."

T.J. felt kind of sheepish. He did, however, understand the basic idea. He suddenly remembered their exchange at the cash register on Saturday. "Mr. McKinney," he asked, "is that why you asked if I had any brushes?"

"Yes, sir," he replied. "A lot of people come in thinking that one tool, in your case the roller, is all they need to get something done. I've found that one tool is usually not enough. You need the right tool for the job...and rollers aren't the right tool to get the edge of a room painted!" Mr. McKinney laughed. "Kinda like people, you need the right person for the job, too. We're not all made the same. Some people are just better at some types of jobs than others." He handed the brush to T.J. "Here, take this. You'll also find this useful," he said as he picked up a small foam brush. As they walked toward the front of the store, Mr. McKinney looked back at T.J. "You look like somethin's got you down. Since everything's OK with Jill and the baby, I'm guessing work." He paused in thought for a minute. "Lackey & Durham is full of all kinds of folks...maybe you've met up with one that's a little hard to deal with." *Is it that transparent?* T.J. wondered. "I've got a challenge for you if you're interested. Why don't you find three people who are like these paint brushes and come tell me about them at Wilder's on Saturday morning?"

T.J. looked a little surprised. "Mr. McKinney, I don't want to waste your time. I really appreciate your help with the room, but I'm sure you have more important things to do on a Saturday morning."

"Nonsense," responded Mr. McKinney, "there's not much could be less important than shooting the breeze over gravy and biscuits on Saturday."

T.J. paid for his brushes and shook Mr. McKinney's hand. "OK, Mr. McKinney, see you Saturday."

# Chapter Eleven

As he walked into the hospital, it almost seemed routine. Jill was in a good mood as she told T.J. about seeing the baby via ultrasound today. "I've been thinking," she said. "We need to figure out what we're going to call this little guy. He's been pretty active today. Maybe he can tell how excited I am to be heading home. Anyway, what about Shawn? I like the way that sounds: Introducing our class valedictorian, Shawn Hughes! It's going, going, gone...another home run for Shawn Hughes."

T.J. had to admit that the second one made him smile. "That's not bad but I would like to use a family name. How about naming him Alfred after my great-grandfather?" Jill looked like someone had just offered her spoiled milk.

"I'd like something a little more modern. What do you say I work on a list tomorrow? I'll start with Shawn and Alfred. So, how was your day?"

T.J. took a deep breath. He wanted to say, "Not bad," and leave it at that, but when he took the time to explain his work situations to Jill, she usually had some pretty wise insight. Ten minutes later, he had explained his frustration with Hoyt and his love of the "standard process." He concluded, "It took him almost three hours to get back with me this morning. I don't know what he was doing...probably another management meeting." T.J. closed his eyes, took a deep breath in, and tried to breathe out his frustrations. As he opened his eyes, he noticed some flowers in the corner of the room with a card. Looking to change the subject, he said, "Nice flowers. Who sent them?"

Jill smiled a half smile. "Well, let's just say that management meetings aren't the only thing that might cause your boss to be late. He and his wife, Ann, came by this morning with the card and flowers. I enjoyed talking to them. You know, they are such nice people. I had a really hard time seeing how the guy I saw this morning could be so frustrating at work."

T.J. looked sheepishly at the floor. He could relate to Jill's problem. Hoyt *was* a nice guy. Sometimes he was too nice, and this time, much nicer than T.J. gave him credit for. But how was it that one person could have so many positives in one area and be so clueless in another? It was almost like the Dr. Jekyll version of Hoyt showed up at the hospital while the Mr. Hyde version showed up at work. Hoyt wasn't evil at work; he just didn't seem to understand how things got done. T.J. didn't want to discuss work or Hoyt any more. Jill, however, wasn't quite done yet. "You know, honey, the more I talked to Hoyt and Ann today, the more I realized that they are good people with good intentions. Do you think Hoyt has good intentions at work?"

To the best of T.J.'s knowledge, Hoyt had never intentionally sabotaged anything. He did care about the people around him. It was as if he had mastered the tools and methodologies in his previous job and he was trying to apply those same things in an arena where they didn't add as much value. What was it that Mr. McKinney had said about having the right tool for the job? He filed that thought away as Jill's dinner came through the door.

"What's on the menu tonight?" Jill asked.

"Meatloaf, squash, a roll, and cherry cobbler," the orderly replied. "Just make sure that you eat the meatloaf first...your baby needs that protein!"

Jill smiled as she took the tray. "Thanks, Anna, you've taken good care of me all day."

"Hey, Dad," Anna continued, "what are you eating tonight?"

It took T.J. a couple of seconds to realize that he was being spoken to. Was he really ready to be called Dad? Bringing himself back to the question at hand, he replied, "Probably a PB and J. No reason to get all those dishes dirty for one. Why do you ask?"

Anna smiled. "That's what I thought. Here, we always have some extra meals, why don't you two eat together?"

T.J. stood to take the tray. "That's very kind of you. Thanks for thinking about me."

"Got to love our neighbor as ourselves; that's what the good book says!" Anna smiled as she slid back toward the door. "You two have a nice night."

# Chapter Twelve

After leaving the hospital, T.J. arrived home on a mission to try out his newfound painting knowledge. As he changed his clothes, he found himself thinking about Mr. McKinney's assessment of his problems. Was there a sign over his head announcing his troubles to the world? And Hoyt coming to the hospital today absolutely knocked him head over heels. He couldn't believe that Hoyt and his wife would take the time out of their day to do that. And then again, he could believe it; he just couldn't easily reconcile it with the behaviors and attitudes he saw at work every day. Maybe, T.J. thought to himself, he was the problem. But he had been so successful and content working for Andy that that thought didn't seem right either. After all, this was the same job he had been in just a year ago and it seemed so much easier then. He sighed, no answers, just more questions. It was time to go paint.

As he entered the baby's room, he looked at the wall he had painted last night. It was a soothing blue. One that he hoped would spark the imagination of his son as he saw it after he woke up every morning. He hoped it would pass the subliminal message to reach for the stars (or at least the clouds) as the little boy looked at it. For now, however, he had a blue sky in a white frame. Mr. McKinney had provided him the solution to that problem so he decided he would try it on the second wall. As he turned to face the second wall, his heart sank a little. For no particular reason, T.J. had started with the wall on the left side of the room as you entered. He now realized that it was the only wall that did not have a door or window frame on it. Hmmm. If Mr. McKinney's technique worked for making straight lines between the ceiling and the wall then he figured it would work for the window staring at him from the other side of the room as well. He shook the paint, opened the paint can, and loaded his brush. After making his reservoir, he pulled his line up to the bottom of the windowsill. Steady, steady, steady...there's the corner, and lift. Wow, that looked straight. T.J. had always liked straight lines and he was particularly proud of this one.

Fifteen minutes later, T.J. had the inverse of the first wall. This one had a blue frame with a white 'picture' which enclosed another blue frame around the window. T.J. stood in the middle of the room admiring the nice straight lines. He had plenty of time to paint the middle, so he filled the roller tray and got to work. After about five minutes, he found himself a little bored. He liked the fact that the roller could cover so much area at once, but he found that he enjoyed the precision needed to get a straight line. It seemed to him that lines required more skill than rolling. At least for him, they required a more enjoyable skill. Maybe T.J. was the right person for the line-painting job but not the rolling job. T.J. caught himself yawning and looked down at his watch. It was getting late and he was definitely the right person for the 'get a good night's sleep' job. Everyone kept warning him that he needed to be caught up on his sleep before the baby arrived. After finishing the wall and cleaning up, he would be glad to oblige.

# Chapter Thirteen

Tuesday morning found T.J. walking into the plant more excited than he'd been in a while. He wasn't looking forward to the 'opportunities' that his job might present but he had challenged himself to find the three types of people Mr. McKinney mentioned. After last night's painting, he had identified himself with the angled brush. He was hoping to find a 'roller' today. As he walked by the indicator board in his shop, he reviewed yesterday's numbers. The TR1 downtime was just killing his team's productivity. He caught a glimpse of movement on his right just before a large hand clamped down on his left shoulder. "Hey, Bossman," said Joey.

Joey Lawson had been working in this shop since T.J. was in kindergarten. He had seen it all. T.J. could always count on him to put things in perspective. "Numbers lookin' rough this week. Can't you get those pencil pushers in Planning to come down here to the floor and see what's possible 'fore they send this junk out?"

T.J. smiled; most of the people in Planning hadn't seen the shop floor in years, if ever. Joey continued, "Well, I'm a gonna make as much as I can make and their fancy charts aren't gonna make me any faster or slower." Joey had consistently been one of the best employees in the shop.

"Thanks, Joey," T.J. said. "I appreciate your perspective. Keep making as much as you can and I'll see what we can do with the pencil pushers."

"Go get 'em, Bossman," Joey said as he turned to go.

Walking down the line, he was reminded about his favorite aspect of the job. The people who worked in his shop were skilled, hardworking, and the backbone of the company. They did 'real' work every day. Not sitting at a desk all day, not management, and definitely not "pencil pushing." The team in the shop had been working together so long that they were more like family than co-workers. T.J.'s job was to listen to the problems that the 'family' was having and resolve as many of them as possible. His team had been dealing with this TR1 issue for almost two weeks and he couldn't fix it. That in and of itself was frustrating, but the fact that Hoyt was not helping to resolve it magnified the feeling of frustration T.J. had.

Between various interruptions for issues as varied as lack of supplies to consulting someone on the team about an insurance question, T.J. spent the rest of the morning updating training records for his team. He heard someone coming down the hall toward his office. As he looked up from the pile of training course completion forms, he heard a knock on his door. Eric Lyons was one of T.J.'s best friends at the company. They had started the same day and worked through several crises together. Until recently, they had eaten lunch together most days. Unfortunately for their lunch schedule, Eric had recently taken a new job which made it more difficult for them to find the time to talk, much less eat together. Not only did Eric's job mean fewer lunches together, the new position, production planning manager, often put he and T.J. at opposite sides of an argument. Regardless of his frustrations with Eric as of late, T.J. was glad to see him.

"Lunch?" Eric asked.

T.J. smiled. "You actually have time? Absolutely!" T.J. enjoyed lunches with Eric because they thought the same way about a lot of things. "Got time to run to the Burger Bar?" said T.J. "Jill's not home until tomorrow so I'm living the wild, carefree life of a bachelor for a few more hours. When do you want to go?" Eric laughed. "Well, maybe now since it's twelve fifteen." T.J. looked up at the clock on the wall. He had been working for two hours straight. He sure felt it as he stood up from his chair.

"You want to drive?" T.J. asked as he reached for his coat. Eric backed out of the doorway to let T.J. reach the coat hook. "I've heard all about your weekend, so in the interest of my personal safety, yes, I'll definitely drive."

# Chapter Fourteen

The Burger Bar had been a fixture in town for over thirty years and it was beginning to show its age. The once-white Formica covering the tabletops was yellowed and chipping, the walls were a curious color of brownish orange, and many of the items adorning the walls wouldn't look out of place in an antiques shop. The customers overlooked all of that, however, for the opportunity to have one of Howard Smith's famous hamburgers. Smitty, as everyone called him, knew everything about everybody in town. As soon as he saw T.J. walk in the door, Smitty did a quarter turn away from the grill to greet him.

"How's your sweet lady doin'?" Smitty asked.

"Just fine, Mr. Smith," T.J. replied. "She's coming home tomorrow. Thanks for asking." T.J. and Eric took a table in the back corner, away from the grill and cash register which was manned by Smitty's wife, Mabel. T.J. felt like this was 'his' table based on the number of times he'd eaten at it. In fact, if he looked under it, he was almost sure that he would find a wad of Big League Chew that he'd stuck there after a baseball game many years ago.

When the waitress came over, she chatted with the men for a few minutes about the weather and Friday night's playoff win by the local high school team, the Chiefs. "Well, boys," she said, "haven't seen you in a while. Guessin' you want the regular?"

Eric smiled and replied, "T.J. convinced me that Smitty made the best burger in the state and I haven't had one yet that proved him wrong!"

She turned toward the grill and hollered at Smitty, "Two regulars, all the way! Now, boys, I'll be right back with your drinks." The Burger Bar only served sweet tea and coffee so drink orders were usually unnecessary based on the time of day you were dining.

"So," Eric began, "we were all so glad to hear that you and Jill were OK after the accident. It could'a been bad." T.J. didn't need reminding. He had run through the possible scenarios a million times in his head.

"It could have but we're sure thankful it wasn't," T.J. replied. "Mama and the little guy are doing well. It'll be nice to get back to normal tomorrow." T.J. changed the subject. "So how are things going for you?"

Eric filled T.J. in on the latest happenings with his family, including the trials of having a three-year-old that was scared of his own room. "You'll never be the same, T.J.," Eric sighed. "It's a wild ride. Fun, yes. But maddening, exhausting, and challenging too. Most days, being a parent makes work look like a breeze!"

As T.J. prepared to respond, he was interrupted by the arrival of their food. A couple of bites into his cheeseburger, T.J. couldn't hold it in any longer. "So what's going on with you guys at work? Is somebody out to get me with these impossible targets?" Eric stared at his fries for a minute before raising his head to meet T.J.'s eyes. "We all know the TR1 is unreliable but my boss won't let me take that into account until he gets a formal request from your department." T.J.'s brow crinkled in thought, then dismay. "Hoyt won't even think about elevating the issue until Friday. He's so shortsighted! It seems like his key management strategy is 'don't rock the boat.' I'm telling you, Eric, I'm frustrated." Eric understood. Everyone liked Andy and his promotion was well deserved. Hoyt seemed like a nice guy, but he didn't have the same approach that Andy did—and T.J. was suffering for it. Eric wanted to help.

"Maybe I can bring up the issue this afternoon in our staff meeting. Hoyt was invited but he said that he couldn't be there."

T.J.'s head snapped up. "I'm not invited but I *can* be there."

# Chapter Fifteen

T.J. squirmed uncomfortably in the broken down blue desk chair that had found its way into the back of the conference room. What was he thinking? The agenda item about the TR1 was at least twenty minutes away and the other topics in the Planning staff meeting were of no interest to him. As he stared at the white, cinder block walls, he began to think that this meeting was actually less interesting than watching paint dry. Paint! He immediately remembered Mr. McKinney's challenge and his goal to find a 'roller' today. Since he had forgotten about that until now, he hadn't made any progress. The thought gave him new hope in staying awake for the next twenty minutes so he began to scribble on his notepad.

**Angled Brush = Lines = Structure = Me**
**Roller = Lots of paint delivered but not much accuracy**
**…therefore needs the structure of the Angled Brush**
**Foam Brush = ?**

He stopped writing as the door to the conference room creaked open. T.J. was surprised to see Hoyt on the other side. "Right on time, Hoyt," said John, Eric's boss. "Glad you could make it." John looked over the rest of the room and said, "OK, y'all know about the problems we've been havin' in Hoyt's group. The TR1 has been up and down for the past two weeks and that sure wasn't in our plans. If you look at our indicator board, you'll see that this problem hasn't hurt our goal of on-time plan delivery at all. But ol' Hoyt here has different objectives than we do. He's got to make sure that he hits those targets we're projecting for his shops. Hasn't been going so well lately, eh, Hoyt? So, I asked him to come talk to us today and see what we could do to help him out."

Hoyt smiled as he looked around the room, until he came to T.J. For a brief moment, his look conveyed confusion, but he recovered quickly before starting. "Thanks, John, for letting T.J. and me come to your staff meeting today. We know that you have a lot of important things to do and we sure don't want to waste any more of your time than necessary." *Too late*, thought T.J. as Hoyt continued. "Now this downtime's been hard on our team. We didn't make our numbers last week and this week's not looking great. Next month, we would really appreciate it if you folks would take into account the fact that we might have some problems." Hoyt smiled as he sat down.

"Thanks, Hoyt," said John. T.J.'s eyes widened as he realized Hoyt didn't plan to say anything else. "Well," John concluded, "that's it for today's meeting. Anything we missed?" T.J.'s eyes caught Hoyt's. The scowl on T.J. face generated a look of surprise from Hoyt. Trying to diffuse the situation, Hoyt smiled back at T.J.

"Excuse me, John," T.J. stood up, "would you mind if I said a couple of things?"

"Absolutely not," drawled John. "We've got six minutes left on this topic."

T.J. knew John was a stickler for time so he glanced at the clock: 3:54 p.m. "Look, I know that planning for this plant is not an easy job." Several heads nodded and T.J. took that as a good sign. "I really appreciate the hard work that you do, but how are you measured?"

One team member looked at T.J. skeptically. "On time delivery of the plan…" his voice faded as though he wanted to say more.

"Right, Joe," responded T.J. "Are any of you measured on how well the plan is met?"

"Of course not," Joe continued, "we can't control whether or not you do your job. Why measure us on something we can't control?" T.J. looked around the room. He was clearly outnumbered, but he was so frustrated by the situation that he was ready to try anything.

"I understand that you can't control our production, but maybe we could share an indicator between the shops and planning…a weekly indicator that measures plan accuracy. Then we could work together to update the plan weekly to avoid issues like we're having now with the TR1."

"What?" bellowed John. "That's the craziest idea I've ever heard. We can't redo those metrics. That would take a plant manager level decision. Look, we'll do everything we can to help you guys out next month but we are not going to change our entire process because of one little problem in your shop!"

As T.J. started to respond, Hoyt jumped in. "Yes, the indicators we have were created for a reason. Let's try to work within the system before we create a whole new one."

T.J. exhaled as he sat down, defeated. The 'way we do things' had won again.

"It's four o'clock," said John, smiling. Thanks for a good meeting today, team. And thanks to Hoyt and T.J. for coming as well. Have a good week."

# Chapter Sixteen

As T.J. left the conference room, he saw Hoyt waiting for him. Hoyt jumped in with a quick "What was that all about?" T.J. had taken all he could. "Hoyt, the process around this is broken and needs to be fixed!" *Anyone with half a brain could see that*, thought T.J. Hoyt looked at T.J. paternally and T.J. half expected him to start the next sentence with "Now, son…" but he didn't.

"T.J., you're an action-oriented guy, but sometimes we can take actions that don't give us the results we're hoping to achieve. Let's not start from scratch because of one problem."

Now that he was out of the conference room, T.J. saw wisdom in that advice. However, he wanted someone to help fix the problem and Hoyt didn't seem to be moving in that direction. Hoyt concluded, "Look, earlier this week you asked me to start pushing on Wednesday based on your Tuesday update. Why don't you drop by my office as you get ready to leave and we'll make a plan of attack." T.J. nodded his agreement. "By the way," Hoyt continued, "I noticed that post two had a couple of tools out of place while Josh, Jay…"

"Joey?" said T.J.

"Yeah, him. Anyway, I noticed that the tools were out of place while he was working. We have to meet the standards, T.J. Take care of it." Hoyt turned to leave and it took everything T.J. had not to send him down the hall a little faster with a swift kick.

T.J. made one last trip around the shop floor to remind his team that he would be off for the rest of the week. He got back to his office and collapsed into his chair. The clock read 4:30 p.m. It was time to go get Jill from the hospital but he had to see Hoyt first. *Plan of attack*, he thought to himself. *I'm not sure Hoyt's ever attacked anything!* He gathered his things and walked down the hall to Hoyt's office. He was hoping for a miracle but planning for a disaster.

Hoyt was on the phone when T.J. arrived so he lightly knocked at the door. Hoyt smiled and waved T.J. to the wooden chair that looked like it was 'original equipment' when the factory was built. The phone conversation was winding down. "OK, John… Yes, yes, I understand…We want to work together with your team as well. OK. Thanks for your time. Have a good evening." Hoyt placed the phone back on the receiver as he turned to talk to T.J. "I guess you know who that was, T.J. And you probably know why we were talking." T.J. looked at the floor, preparing himself for another lecture on why there were processes and standards and how he didn't respect them. But it didn't happen. The silence lasted two seconds then five, then ten. T.J. looked up at Hoyt. "T.J., you were right about the need to share indicators. I really think that your idea is great! But you can't surprise me like that, much less John. I thought he was going to have a heart attack!" T.J. allowed himself a half smile. John was pretty angry.

T.J. responded, "OK, Hoyt, what am I supposed to do? They determine the targets, and I have to try to meet them…regardless of the feasibility. It's crazy!"

T.J.'s words hung in the air for what seemed like forever. When Andy was confronted with a problem like this, he immediately started drawing pictures.

T.J. took a step out the door and grabbed a sheet of paper from the scrap paper pile on the hallway table. Pulling a pen from his back pocket, he sat down at the small table in Hoyt's office and started to sketch the organization.

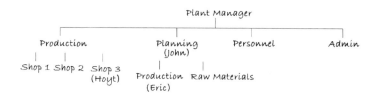

He circled Production and Planning. "In the meeting today, we can see that these two departments need to share an objective. Today, planning is measured on completing their plan on time and we're measured on how much of the plan we complete." Hoyt nodded. T.J. took that as a good sign and forged ahead. "I really think that we should both be measured on how well we achieve the plan if we can agree how that's measured. We'll also need to measure our production, just like we do today, to communicate the shop results."

Hoyt seemed to buy into the plan. "OK, T.J.," he said, "I understand where you're going here. It's getting late and I've got to head out. We've got a planning meeting for next year's Little League season."

Hoyt had coordinated the local Little League as long as anyone could remember and it always ran like clockwork. "Go get Jill and take a couple of days to relax. In Friday's Shop Staff meeting, we'll talk about improving the accuracy of our plans and how we could measure something like that."

T.J. looked at the clock: 4:54. He was going to be later than he planned and he didn't have any more energy to give the topic. "Thanks, Hoyt," he sighed, "That's a start."

# Chapter Seventeen

T.J. pulled into the hospital parking lot at 5:15. Later than planned but not so late that Jill would be frustrated—at least that's what he was hoping. When he started down the hall to room 105, he was surprised to see a smiling Jill in a wheelchair. "Hey, honey," T.J. started, "sorry I'm late."

Jill reached up to hug him. "Let's hit the road...I've had enough hospital life for a while!"

A nurse T.J. didn't recognize handed him Jill's overnight bag. "Mr. Hughes, if you'll pull around to the front, we'll meet you there and you can take this lovely lady home."

*With pleasure*, thought T.J.

Tuesday evening was uneventful. After dinner on the couch, T.J. and Jill curled up together to watch *Jeopardy!* and channel surfed until bedtime. They were so happy to be home together that they didn't need to say much...or have much to say. T.J. woke up the next morning and squinted his eyes. What in the world was wrong? Why had he overslept? The sun was out! He turned his head to look at the clock. It was 8:45! He jumped out of the bed and headed for the shower. As he was leaving the room, he turned to look at the clock one last time and noticed Jill, still sound asleep. *Oh yeah*, he thought, *no work today*. He smiled a grateful smile, shook his head a little, grabbed some clothes, and headed to the bathroom.

By the time Jill got up at 9:30, he had taken a shower and was washing the few dishes he had used during the week. T.J. greeted his cute and pregnant wife with a "Hey, sleepyhead!" as she appeared in the kitchen doorway. Jill smiled weakly as she pulled out a chair at the kitchen table. "I could get used to that," she said. "Nobody waking me up in the middle of the night to check on me, a soft bed, breakfast when I want it..."

The implication was not missed by T.J. "Yep, we've got you covered right here. We have a vast array of breads and cereals from the finest stores in town!" T.J. reached in the pantry to pull out a loaf of bread and some raisin bran. "Fruits from around the world!" he said, as he delivered a couple of bananas to the table. "And finally, the freshest dairy products!" He opened the fridge to reveal a half-gallon of milk and some butter. "What can I get for you today, Madame?"

She smiled. "You're silly and we have to go to the store. What have you been eating?" Jill picked up a banana and started to peel it. "So, other than the store, what did you have planned for today, Mr. Waiter?"

They discussed the plan for the day over breakfast. A visit to the grocery store was definitely in order. T.J. wanted to take a look at the gutters, as they seemed full after this year's bumper crop of leaves. Finally, they agreed that they wanted to finish the baby's room.

As she was leaving the kitchen, Jill stopped in the doorway of the half-painted blue room. "T.J.," she gushed, "this looks great! You didn't tell me you had already started!"

He smiled. "I was hoping to be done when you got back but I had a few lessons to learn about painting."

Jill's mind was working, "Do you think that we could finish it this week? Then we could have the crib up and the room decorated by the end of the year!"

T.J. rolled his eyes and sighed in mock protest. "Weren't you just in the hospital?" he asked. Although she had a new goal, Jill was still a little weak, so they agreed that T.J. would run errands before lunch and Jill would rest during the afternoon while T.J. worked outside. They would take a look at the room together that night.

# Chapter Eighteen

Before dinner, T.J. and Jill made a quick visit to the baby's room. While Jill sat on a stool mentally organizing the room, T.J. explained the painting lessons he had learned during the week. He finished with, "I think that I can have the room done tomorrow. Hopefully, I'll have a revelation about the roller and foam brush types too."

Jill jumped in, "So you say that you're an angled brush." *She is listening,* T.J. thought. "I can see that. You like plans and structure. You even fold your trash into squares before throwing it away! So let's take someone like Andy, what's he?"

T.J. grimaced and closed his eyes. "I don't know. The roller can move a lot of paint but it's not very accurate. I never thought of Andy as having problems with accuracy. He and I were always able to come to a solution and move on it quickly. Hoyt's obviously the opposite of Andy but I don't see him as a roller...he doesn't move much paint at all!" T.J. opened his eyes to see Jill smiling up at him.

"Sounds like you're close, Mr. Painter. I think that a couple more hours with these paint fumes will give you all kinds of great ideas!"

Jill looked at the floor. It was as if she wanted to say something else but wasn't quite sure how. "T.J., I'd really like to try to go visit the bank on Friday afternoon."

T.J. was surprised. "When's the last time you talked to Dave?"

"Well, I talked to him yesterday and he said to take my time, but honestly, today was kind of boring. There's only so much *Price is Right* a girl can watch!" T.J. laughed. That was one of his favorite daytime shows too.

"So you're tired of watching Plinko chips and being reminded to spay and neuter pets that we don't have...that's fair. I guess you have to find out if you're ready. What do you say we eat lunch at the Italian Garden on Friday and I'll drop you off afterward?"

"Deal," she replied. She reached out her hand to pull him close and give him a hug. "Thanks for being so understanding."

As they were discussing the baby's room, the doorbell rang. T.J. looked down at his watch. Who in the world was at their door at 5:32 p.m. on a Wednesday night? T.J. walked to the door and snuck a look out the living room window to see three women who looked like they were getting ready to feed an army. He opened the door to see Martha McKinney and two other parishioners from McKinney's Chapel carrying as much food as he and Jill ate in a week. "Good evening, ladies!" T.J. said, as he tried to disguise the fact he had forgotten about their visit. "Please come in from the cold."

"No, sir, Mr. T.J. Hughes, we're not here to visit, just came to drop off a few things for you and your cute little wife to eat while she gets better." Martha McKinney's voice hadn't changed since T.J. first heard it at age nine. "Now, we're just going to give this to you and get right on out of here. Emily, Amy, you just load ol' T.J. up."

After five minutes of storage and re-warming instructions, Martha and her friends were on their way to McKinney's Chapel for the evening service.

Jill walked into the living room after the door closed. "It sounds like someone wanted to help out an injured, pregnant mother-to-be." She and T.J. laughed as they moved the food into the kitchen. It all smelled wonderful and would last them over a week. For dinner, they enjoyed some chicken and mashed potatoes followed by a slice of red velvet cake. They spent a few minutes writing thank you notes and decided that they were both ready for bed.

On Thursday morning, T.J. woke up early, ate a couple of cookies for breakfast, and went in to paint. As he shook the paint, he thought about his conversation with Jill the night before. If Andy and Hoyt were opposites, then which one was a roller and which was a foam brush? One of the things that he said to Jill kept coming back to him. "*I never thought of Andy as having problems with accuracy. He and I were always able to come to a solution and move on it quickly.*" Why did T.J. think of him and Andy as a unit when he thought about accuracy? He poured the blue paint into the tray. It looked tasty, even at 7:15 in the morning.

He pulled the angled brush out of its protective cardboard sleeve. The fine folks at the Builder's Best line had made a soft, brown brush with a glossy, brown handle. Even T.J., no paintbrush expert, could appreciate the quality.

He dipped the brush into the paint and began his 'paint reservoir' above the kickboard. Ten minutes later, he had a nice blue line. He kept replaying his conversation with Jill in his head: "*He and I were always able to come to a solution and move on it quickly.*" T.J. moved the ladder to the corner to begin painting the line between the ceiling and the wall. As he painted, he thought about a couple of the successes he and Hoyt had experienced: the installation of the new machine in the shop and the addition of per item incentive pay for his team. He and Andy would sit for hours. Andy would throw out an idea and T.J would smooth out the edges. T.J. was making a frame that Andy's ideas would fit into so they could be implemented.

*That's it!* he thought, as he snapped his head up. "Ow!" he yelled as his head hit the ceiling. *Oh yeah*, he thought, *I am on a ladder.* He got down, rubbed the sore spot on the back of his head, and looked up to see if his hard head had damaged the ceiling plaster.

Before he moved the ladder, he sat down on the floor and began talking to no one in particular. "So, if I'm an angled brush, Andy was a roller! He came up with the main ideas and then I provided the structure to focus and implement them. That's why we were successful together. Sometimes, Andy would show up with a crazy idea but when we zoomed in on the actionable part," T.J. made a rectangular frame out of his hands like a movie director, "we were able to get things done. Andy's ideas were always good, they just needed a little focus...and that was my role."

Jill appeared in the doorway, rubbing the sleep from her eyes. "Honey, who are you talking to? It sounds like you're pretty excited about something. Did you figure out what type of brush Andy is?"

"I think so," T.J. said with a smile. "Can I tell you about it over some toast?"

# Chapter Nineteen

T.J. excitedly explained his hypothesis to Jill over breakfast. "Sounds logical to me," she said with a smile. "Would you please pass the butter?" She added a pat to her last bite of toast. "So how long have you been up?"

"Not too long," T.J. replied. "I think I can finish painting and clean up by lunchtime."

Jill's face lit up. "Oooo. I'm going to get out the baby clothes your sister sent us and start going through them. Maybe we could start putting the furniture together this weekend!"

"Do you still want to go back to work tomorrow?" T.J. asked.

"I think so," she said. "I dreamt that I was at my desk and I heard a customer at the front desk talking about paintbrushes. I woke up and realized it was you! So, I figure that 'real work' might be a good diversion. And I felt pretty good when I woke up this morning. I think a half-day this week will be good preparation for next week." She pushed her chair back from the table and pushed her round belly up from the chair. "OK, Mr. Painter. I'm heading to the shower. I'll come by to see if you've had any revelations when I get out."

As T.J walked back into the baby's room, he went over to take a closer look at the two walls that were already painted. He ran his hand over one of them to feel the smoothness of the blue paint. *What's this?* he thought to himself. There was a small, round, black hole on the wall. It looked like someone had removed a nail or push pin. As he looked more closely at the wall, he could see several holes. He imagined that this could have been the location of a poster featuring a child's favorite sports player. He walked over to the unpainted walls. Sure enough, he found twelve similar holes. T.J. knew that he needed to fill them before he painted, so he headed out to the shed to get the spackle and putty knife.

After ten minutes, he had filled all of the holes in the white walls but not the ones in the blue walls. He was certain that the small white circles would stand out like a whole handful of sore thumbs on the blue background so it was clear he had to paint them. *How?* he wondered to himself as he looked at the floor. Certainly the roller was not the right tool to paint spots so small. It would deliver much more paint than needed. He looked down at the angled brush. *Maybe it could work…*, he thought, but it would still not be focused enough. He needed something that would put a really small amount of paint in a really specific area. Something like a cotton swab or, his eyes lit up when he noticed the brown bag on the other side of the room, or a foam brush! T.J. got more and more excited as he filled in the holes. The foam brush wasn't necessary at the start of the project. You needed a roller to make its wide strokes and the angled brush to create some boundaries. However, to ensure that the room looked 'as good as new' after some bumps, dings, and holes, the foam brush was crucial!

While the spackle dried on the other walls, T.J. rolled the paint onto the third wall. As he painted, he thought about what a 'foam brush' might look like in day-to-day life. He could imagine someone who was very concerned about the details and whose focus on the details might lead them to miss big things right in front of them. It was as though he could hear the brush saying, "Do you see how obvious it is that there's a problem here? There's a white spot right here on this wall! If I don't paint this spot, nobody else will. I don't want to hear about any other work you have for me to do until I fix this white spot right here. I'll let you know when I'm ready for you to show me where the next one is. This is my kind of job and I'm good at it, but don't start talking 'bout painting this whole wall. That would take forever!" He laughed to himself when he realized that the 'voice' of the foam brush had been Hoyt's. When he was done rolling the wall, he stepped back to admire his work.

Jill snuck in the room and stood beside him, wrapping her arm around his waist. "Figure anything out?"

"Yes, I think so," T.J. said. "Hoyt has a completely different focus than Andy. He's so focused on the details that my 'frame' seems much too big to him. Andy was so focused on the big picture that my 'frames' seemed too small for him! Now I just have to figure out how to convince Hoyt that painting the spackle spots isn't the only thing that matters!"

Jill looked at T.J. and raised her eyebrows. "Are you sure that you haven't spent too much time painting in a poorly ventilated area?"

T.J. smiled. "Maybe so, but I only have one more wall to do, so why don't you come back in a little while and I'll explain it all after I've gone completely crazy!"

# Chapter Twenty

T.J. whistled as he edged the last wall and doorframe, thinking about what he had learned. It was clear that Andy and Hoyt were different but now he better understood why and what they were focused on. He and Andy had successfully worked together but Andy had always been the 'big thinker.' T.J.'s role was to rein him at the right place (in private) and at the right time (as early as possible). He and Hoyt had seen a few successes as well...but T.J. had been the initiator. With Hoyt, T.J. had gone through several excruciating (for him at least) sessions where they had reviewed everything about a project in much more detail than T.J. thought necessary. Looking back, T.J. saw that Andy had probably suffered though some similar sessions with him. "No, Andy, we have to take Joe's availability into account. We won't be done with the project as early as you want." The pieces of the puzzle were coming together in his head.

He finished the last line parallel to the ceiling and looked at the blue 'frame.' It clearly needed some art-work. T.J. painted a smiley face on the left side of the wall which quickly became two big smiley faces and one little one. He stepped back and smiled at their first 'family portrait.'

"Wow, you've become Picasso!" Jill laughed as she came into the room. "The little guy looks pretty happy. I just wish we had a name for him." She closed her eyes in thought. "Have you come up with any?" T.J. smiled. "Honestly, the names I've been thinking about for the past hour have been Andy and Hoyt and I don't think either one of those fits."

"Probably not," she snickered. "The room looks good!" Jill said as she looked around. "How do left-overs sound for lunch?" Martha and her friends from McKinney's Chapel had really outdone themselves and both T.J. and Jill looked forward to the chance to sample another dish they had brought.

"Give me about thirty minutes," T.J. said. "I'll let you know when I'm finished and, if you're ready, we can eat."

"OK," Jill said, "I've got a 'Showcase Showdown' to watch. I'll be waiting for your invitation!"

T.J. picked up the angled brush to touch up one of the 'frame' lines. As he did that, he had a thought. Using the brush, he painted a rendition of the current indicator board in the shop. He put the weekly production numbers in the upper left corner, weekly actions in the upper right corner, monthly numbers in the bottom left, and yearly progress actions in the bottom right, so that it looked like this:

| Wkly Production | Wkly Progress Actions |
|---|---|
| Mthly Production | Yrly Progress Actions |

He painted an arrow and then a blank rectangle about the same size. He divided the rectangle into five sections and labeled them with the things he needed to look at every week: what was planned, what was made, and the actions he needed to do to improve those numbers that week.

| Weekly | |
|---|---|
| **Results (# per day)** | **Actions** |
| **Plan (# per day)** | **Actions** |

Every work area currently posted the weekly plan, so including it on a shared board would just give him the opportunity to review it with the team every day. *That will take care of the short term*, he thought. T.J. then created another rectangle with six sections that he labeled as follows:

| Monthly | |
|---|---|
| **Production** | **Plan** |
| Yearly | |
| **Production** | **Plan** |

If he wanted to keep his job, T.J. would definitely need to make sure that the production numbers kept up with the plan over time! But, it still felt like he was missing something. Where was the shared indicator with Planning? He placed in the word *Achieved* after *Plan* on the weekly board so that now it looked like this:

| Weekly | |
|---|---|
| Results (# per day) | Actions |
| Plan ~~(# per day)~~ Achieved | Actions |

He stepped back to get a different view of the situation and think a little. So what would "Plan Achieved" look like? First, it wouldn't be a number; it would be a percentage. Clearly, a high percentage would reflect positively on both his department and Planning. How would it work? If Production could provide input to Planning by Wednesday, they could finalize the plan on Thursday and, when the production week started on Friday morning, everyone would be ready to execute. If he could have input at that point in the process, he would be more than happy to commit to achieving the plan. "Not bad," he said to no one in particular.

Now, T.J. was excited. This would definitely result in a more reasonable plan for his shop, but how could he convince the Planning department that including the latest downtime information would help them too? Maybe he could get Eric to run a four-week test with him. Then, if all went well, he and Eric could present the results to Hoyt and John for implementation in the rest of the plant. He looked down at his watch. It was almost noon. He would call Eric after lunch and see if there was any hope of getting a test in place for this week. He set the angled brush aside, filled the roller with paint, and rolled the paint onto the last wall and over his indicator boards. As he obscured the last remaining white stripe, the floor creaked behind him. "Ooooh," Jill said, "it looks great! T.J. Hughes, you are an excellent painter."

"Thanks," T.J. replied. "I never knew that there was so much to painting a room. Want to help me clean up?"

# Chapter Twenty-One

T.J explained his painting revelations to Jill over their lunch of leftovers.

"So let me summarize," she said. "Hoyt's a foam brush. His focus is maintaining things. You're an angled brush, focused on building a frame. Andy is a roller, laying out a big-picture vision but maybe not so accurate."

T.J. had a revelation. "Great summary, I need to go look through the trash for a minute." Jill gave him a puzzled look. "I'll be right back," he said, as the door slammed behind him. Five minutes later he returned to the kitchen and placed the wrapper from the rollers in the center of the table. The blue 'Vision' brand stood out on the white background. Beside it, he laid the cardboard wrap from the angled brush. It proudly declared 'Builder's Best' in red and white. Finally, he laid the still-damp foam brush on the table. He turned it over to show the 'Mr. Maintenance' brand on its handle. "Jill, you're amazing! I didn't realize that the brands were giving me a clue." He wondered aloud, "Does this model fit everyone?"

Jill laughed. "Well, I definitely see myself as a builder. I like new challenges, but I do best when someone gives me general direction. Once a challenge is met, I am ready for a new one."

T.J. decided to try the model out on his parents. His mother was a teacher. Being fulfilled by teaching the same grade for twenty-five years seemed like a difficult thing for a visionary or builder to do. "So," T.J. said aloud, "what about my mom? She's been teaching first graders for twenty-five years. She's really good at it but that would drive me crazy. You think she's a maintainer?"

Jill looked up slowly, "Nope, builder...just a builder of *people* instead of a builder of *things*."

T.J.'s eyes widened. "Oh," he said, "you're right. At the end of the year, she's always so proud of what her students have learned and the fact that they are ready for the next grade. So, how about Dad?" T.J. asked. "He's always loved being a dentist but the thought of seeing the same teeth every six months for the rest of my life gives me the creeps. He especially enjoys the patients that he has been seeing since they were kids. It's like he sees the long-term results of his work in their mouth!"

"Maintainer," Jill said. "He loves that powder-blue 1965 Mustang too. He just enjoys taking care of the car. He's not looking for a new one to rebuild or even a recent model with all the bells and whistles. He wants to keep 'Betsy's' engine clean and running well."

"OK," said T.J, "one more test. How about Shawn and Whitney?" The couple had befriended T.J. and Jill since they had arrived in town and had been true friends.

Jill began, "Shawn's always got a project or two going, and he's interested in trying new things."

"You know, Whitney usually has a pretty extensive 'honey-do' list going as well," T.J. added. "Also, it seems like Shawn's been working in architecture and construction his whole life. He just took over the contracting side of his dad's company a few years ago and you can't drive anywhere with him without him telling you about the homes and businesses they've built in the area. Sounds like a builder to me."

Jill nodded, "OK, let's talk about Whitney. She's a stay-at-home mom and really loves it. I'm guessing she spends her day just trying to keep order in her house. Maintainer?" Jill guessed.

T.J. pondered that idea for a minute. "I was thinking that maintainers were more focused on keeping things running smoothly than coming up with big changes. Seems to me that she's the source of Shawn's to-do list!"

"Yeah," Jill said, "you're right, she does really enjoy coming up with projects to do with their kids, and she is future-oriented. She once told me that her parenting philosophy is to ask, 'Will it matter in twenty years?'"

"Wow," T.J. said, "sounds like a visionary to me."

"So what are you going to do with these revelations?" Jill asked.

"Well, I had an idea about my indicator problem while I was painting the last wall so, for starters, I'm going to call Eric this afternoon to try and get something moving this week. I think I may go into work tomorrow afternoon, too. Now that I understand Hoyt a little better, maybe I can figure out a way to use our strengths together on this issue." T.J. stopped. "Thanks for talking this through with me. I think I'm ready to see Mr. McKinney on Saturday."

Jill smiled, "I think you are, too."

# Chapter Twenty-Two

On Thursday afternoon, T.J. called Eric to discuss testing the Plan Achievement indicator for the next three weeks. After a long discussion, Eric agreed. Since it was already Thursday afternoon, T.J.'s next mission was to convince him to have the Production Planning team talk to Joey so they could include projected downtime in next week's plan. Eric knew that it would be a difficult conversation to have with his team, but T.J. was so passionate about it that he was willing to try. T.J. ended the conversation by scheduling a meeting with Eric on Friday afternoon to discuss the results.

Friday morning dawned gray and overcast and T.J. was out of bed ninety minutes before Jill started moving. He passed the time unboxing the baby's crib and reviewing the instructions. By the time Jill showed up, he had the parts of the bed arranged on the floor and the tools he needed to put the bed together. As they ate breakfast, they agreed to work together on the crib and hang some of the "baby jungle" decorations that Jill's parents had purchased off the registry. The morning passed quickly and, before they knew it, it was time to clean up and head to lunch.

At the Italian Garden, they talked about their week over a couple of slices of pepperoni. Their experience on Saturday had given them and their families a scare, but Jill seemed to be recovering quickly.

"What did you think about while you were in the hospital?" T.J. asked.

Jill's answer surprised him. "You know, I'm really not sure. I remember you coming to see me the first couple of days, but I guess the first thing I clearly remember is Hoyt's visit. As soon as he came through the door, it was like my senses were on full alert for the first time in days. I guess the medicine they put me on kept the baby where he was supposed to be but I feel like I lost a couple of days in return. Jill looked over at T.J. "Were you scared?"

"Yeah," T.J. nodded, "Saturday was pretty awful. I imagined having to call your parents to tell them we'd lost both of you. I didn't know how I was going to survive alone. Then, once I came to the hospital, I was pretty sure you were going to be OK. I knew that the baby wasn't out of the woods yet, but I figured that at least we would have each other."

They sat in silence for a couple of minutes. "So, are we ready for this kid?" T.J. asked.

"I hope so," Jill replied. "Everyone keeps saying to enjoy the time before he gets here and to get plenty of sleep. I know our lives are going to change; I believe it's for the better. Realistically, I don't know how we'll react, but I'm ready to hold him in my arms and sing *Hush, Little Baby* like my mom did to me." "You'll be a great mom," T.J. said, smiling. "What's your biggest fear?"

"I'm still not sure how I will balance being a mom and working. I'm glad I don't have to deal with that question for a couple of months. I really like my job. I mean, I'm ready to go back to work this afternoon. I don't dread it at all. But I've always wanted to be a mother, too." Her voice trailed off and T.J. filled the silence. "I'm just scared I won't know what to do. I like kids and all that, but babies are a different story. Diapers, diaper rash, bottles, baths...all that's new to me. It's like we're going to baby school! Do we get a diploma when it's over? And how do we know if we even passed?"

Jill reached across the table to take her husband's hand. "We'll figure that out together."

T.J. dropped Jill off at the bank, giving her a kiss after walking her to the door. "See you about five?" he asked.

"Yep, sounds good," Jill replied. "I'm just trying to catch up a little today. Love you," she said, as she gave T.J. a peck on the cheek.

T.J. watched as she went through the two sets of glass doors and into the bank. He breathed a thankful prayer and headed back to the car. Ten minutes later, he arrived in the parking lot at the plant. After going through the gate, he planned to see Eric before spending some time on the floor with his team. T.J. dropped off his coat in his office, put on his safety shoes, and headed left out the door toward the Planning department. His feet seemed heavy and he looked down at the large, steel toes that his feet had forgotten in a few short days. He looked up just in time to avoid running into Joey.

"Hey, Bossman!" Joey said with a smile. "How's the little lady?" T.J. couldn't help thinking that a very pregnant Jill would *hate* being called a "little lady."

"Much better, Joey, thanks for asking. She went into work this afternoon so I figured I'd come see your smiling face!"

"Well, glad to hear she's better," Joey said. "Hey, Bossman, you got a minute?"

"Sure, Joey, what's wrong? Do you want to go somewhere we can talk?"

"Nothing's wrong but yeah, we got something to talk about. Come out here on the floor with me." As they walked, T.J. noticed they were headed to the team area, not Joey's post. He was surprised as Joey stopped right in front of the indicator board.

"Bossman, you know what happened yesterday? Lori from Planning came to see me, right out here on the shop floor! She was even wearing safety shoes instead of caps. Anyway, after the shock wore off, we started talking. Do you know what she wanted?" Joey didn't pause long enough for a response. "She asked what machines were down. Said that she was putting together our weekly plan and wanted to make sure that her machine availability was correct. You could have knocked me over with a feather."

T.J. tried to act surprised. "So what did you tell her?"

"I told her about the TR1 and when we hoped to have it back up. We talked about who was going to be here next week. I was so excited I would have told her my bank account balance if I thought it would help. Then, this morning, she came out with a plan for the week that I think we can meet! That's something that'll make me want to come to work on Monday!"

# Chapter Twenty-Three

T.J. knew that Wilder's filled up pretty early on Saturday mornings and Mr. McKinney always opened his store at 8:00 a.m. So, he grudgingly set his alarm clock for 6:30 before going to bed on Friday night. The alarm clock did its job perfectly and it was still dark when T.J. rolled into the parking lot of a standalone wooden building with a green-and-white painted sign over the door proudly declaring the building to be "Wilder's Restaurant." There were pickup trucks of all makes and models filling the parking lot. T.J. felt small as he pulled Jill's Accord into a spot between two of them.

The light coming from the large windows of the building was cheery and warm and made T.J. think of the good food being cooked inside.

He opened the door and surveyed the room full of a mostly a sixty-five and older crowd. Some little ones that appeared to be grandkids were sprinkled around two or three tables. On his second pass of the room, he saw Mr. McKinney in the back corner, as far away from the door as possible, reading the newspaper with a cup of coffee nearby. He looked up as T.J. approached the table.

"Good morning, T.J. Nice of you to join me!" Mr. McKinney reached out his hand. T.J. took it and felt for a minute like he was eleven years old and meeting the kind man for the first time as he was welcomed to the team.

"Have a seat and Amber will be here in just a minute to take your order. So, how's your beautiful wife doing?" T.J. explained Jill's progress and how excited they both were that she would be able to go back to work on Monday. He also took the opportunity to thank Mr. McKinney for the food provided by the ladies of McKinney's Chapel. "That Martha," Mr. McKinney smiled, "she is one amazing cook. She doesn't know how to do anything half-way. I know that she was a blessing to you because she is one to me every day."

He was interrupted by the arrival of the waitress who smiled at T.J. as she came alongside the table. T.J. guessed that Mr. McKinney was one of her 'regulars.'

"Amber, I'd like to introduce you to my friend T.J.," Mr. McKinney began. "I've known him since he was a little feller." Amber and T.J. nodded politely to each other.

"Ready to order?" she asked. T.J. hadn't so much as looked at the menu but he didn't want to waste any time.

"Sure," he responded, "as long as you start with Mr. McKinney first.

"So, Reid," she started, "Saturday morning special with extra gravy and sausage?"

"Yes, ma'am," Mr. McKinney replied. "Why mess with perfection?" he said with a smile. Yes, T.J. thought, he's a regular here all right. He had no idea what a Saturday morning special included but he figured everything would be good.

"Make it two," T.J. said, folding his menu and handing it back, "and a water too, please."

"Anything to drink?" the pleasant young woman asked.

"Just water, thanks."

"Thanks, y'all. I'll be back in a jiffy with your water," she said, pointing her pen at T.J.

"Well, T.J.," Mr. McKinney began, "I'm guessing you had a good week. You look like someone took a load off of your shoulders."

"Yes, sir. Getting Jill home sure helped, but I learned a lot while painting this week, too."

Mr. McKinney jumped in, "Tell me, did you finish your baby's room?"

T.J beamed, "Yes, sir, we did and it looks great. Jill loves it and I think that the baby will too. I definitely needed all three types of brushes to get the end result I wanted."

"Well that's good news," Mr. McKinney responded. "I like to hear about it when somebody achieves their goal."

T.J. continued, "Not only did we get the room painted, but I also had some situations at work that made finding people like the roller and brushes a pretty interesting exercise." T.J. pulled a small plastic bag onto the table from the chair beside him. In front of Mr. McKinney, T.J. placed the blue and white 'Vision' roller wrapper, the red-and-white cardboard wrap from the angled brush declaring 'Builder's

Best,' and the foam brush with the 'Mr. Maintenance' brand on its handle.

Amber returned with T.J.'s water and noticed the painting wrappers and supplies on the table. "You two going to paint something today?" she asked with a smile.

Mr. McKinney answered with a twinkle in his eye, "Nope, T.J. here's done painting; we're going to talk about what he learned."

Amber raised an eyebrow and replied, "You can learn a lot of things when you're painting. My husband and I just repainted our little girl's room. He likes to call it 'Pepto-Bismol Pink.' We sure do learn a little something every time. I'll be back with your food in a few minutes. Y'all let me know if you need anything." With that, she left to visit another table.

Mr. McKinney turned toward T.J. "Well, did you find someone who represents all three types of brushes?"

T.J. nodded. "I sure did. It took a little more work than I thought, but I found people that had the same strengths as each type."

T.J. took a deep breath and began to explain what he had learned. "My old boss, Andy, is just like the roller. He can really see the big picture and talks in generalities a lot. Like the roller, he can cover a lot of 'wall' in a short period of time, but he's not interested in the details. I really liked working with him but I never really understood why until now. I found out that I'm like the angled brush. I love 'making a frame' around things. Andy would make big proposals and I would draw the frame to keep him 'inside the lines.' Although I really enjoyed working with Andy, I've been having a really hard time with Hoyt, my new boss. Now I understand that he's like the foam brush. He focuses on small details that are necessary for a good finished product but is not looking at the big picture." T.J. stopped to take a breath and caught Mr. McKinney's eyes. They were twinkling as he smiled at T.J. like a proud father. The corner of T.J.'s mouth raised in a half smile as he recognized the same look in the old man's eyes that he saw when he learned to hit a curve ball.

Seconds later, Amber arrived with their food. "Well, T.J.," said Mr. McKinney, "let's not let this good food get cold." T.J. looked down at his plate filled with two enormous biscuits, a large bowl of gravy, and two sausage patties. He might not need to eat another meal all day! T.J. unwrapped his utensils and looked up just in time to notice Mr. McKinney's bowed head rising and his eyes opening to look at his food. They both ate in silence for a minute then Mr. McKinney continued. "It seems like you learned a lot about painting, brushes, and people. When I started at Lackey & Durham right out of college, I had some of the same frustrations as you." T. J. was surprised. He had never imagined that Mr. McKinney ever worked anywhere other than the hardware store. T.J. forced his focus back on the conversation in time to hear Mr. McKinney continue. "Lackey & Durham wasn't as big then but I quickly found out that not everyone thought the same way I did. One Sunday afternoon, as I was explaining my problems to my daddy, he took me to the store and gave me a lesson on people and paintbrushes that I never forgot.

"Soon after our talk, I realized that Daddy was a visionary with big dreams for the store but he needed some help...someone to put structure to his ideas. I left the plant a few weeks later, joined Daddy at the store, and never looked back." T.J. was pleased that he had learned the lesson Mr. McKinney wanted to teach him and, at the same time, felt like he was missing something.

"So, Mr. McKinney," T.J. began, "I'm sure you've seen people of all types at your store, church, even when you were at Lackey & Durham. Is one type more successful than the others?"

Mr. McKinney laughed. "Actually, I've seen all types fail equally. And it's usually because they thought they could go it alone. From what I've seen, success happens when you work with the other types."

Mr. McKinney paused to eat a bite and T.J. thought for a minute about Mr. McKinney's claim. He grabbed a napkin from the dispenser and wrote, *Relationships = Success.* "So, Mr. McKinney," T.J. said as he wrote hastily on the napkin, "based on your experiences, how can I best identify and work with each type?"

Mr. McKinney chewed thoughtfully. "Daddy spent some time in Japan after the second World War. It was there that he learned one of his favorite quotes: 'Vision without action is a daydream. Action without vision is a nightmare.' That's one of the best explanations I've heard to explain the relationship between all three types of people. To be successful, you can't have one without the others. Visionaries get a lot of publicity, for example, because they appear to see into the future. In fact, they don't seem to live in the present at all. Did you know that when Winston Churchill was seventeen, he predicted that he would save England? That was forty-nine years before the start of World War Two! Clearly, he was already looking at what the future held for him. Visionaries typically have great charisma and people who 'buy in' to their visions will do almost anything for them. However, their most frequent downfall is that they don't see many (if any) reasons why their vision can't be accomplished. Once the vision is birthed in them, they believe so strongly in it that they are not easily dissuaded, regardless of the information surrounding them. That can be positive like Franklin Roosevelt and the New Deal. That can also be negative like Robert E. Lee at Gettysburg. He didn't listen to the team of generals surrounding him who told him that the battle actually couldn't be won."

T.J. had been listening with such rapt attention that he hadn't taken a bite. He ate several large forkfuls before asking another question. "So do visionaries have an obligation to use their 'special powers' for good?" Mr. McKinney nodded. "Absolutely! A good vision doesn't exist just to make the life of just one person better; it's got to make a difference for humanity. Ever heard of Jim Jones? He convinced over nine hundred people to move with him from the US to 'Jonestown,' Guyana. Then, he was so persuasive that most of them committed suicide at his direction. Was he a visionary? Yes. Did he make a positive difference for humanity? I don't think so."

T.J. sat at the table in stunned silence. How did this small-town hardware store owner come up with such a detailed model of how people act? He took another bite before asking "What about builders? What makes them tick?"

Mr. McKinney smiled. "You're one. You tell me!"

T.J.'s eyes widened as he felt like a spotlight had just turned toward him. "Well, um, builders really like structure. Like visionaries, they, um, look toward the future because they are trying to create something. But, they also have a foot firmly planted in the present because, you know, they are trying to create something today that will be useful tomorrow." T.J.'s eyes sparkled as he remembered one of his favorite builders. He began talking faster. "As a kid, I was fascinated by outer space and those who traveled there. I remember watching that grainy footage of Neil Armstrong walking on the moon and thinking how amazing it was that humans had figured out how to visit space. Why was Armstrong there? Two people made it happen. A visionary named Kennedy pointed the way to the moon in 1961 after only one American had ever been in space. Kennedy wasn't a rocket scientist, but Werner Von Braun was. Von Braun had been building rockets since the 1940s. Von Braun's knowledge plus Kennedy's commitment and vision combined to create a program that could put humans on the moon."

T.J. continued, "Builders are less idea people and more people who 'buy in' to a vision and help make it a reality. They might build things like roads or processes or software. They also build relationships and can serve as the center of a network. Those builders are the type of person that doesn't know the answer… but they know somebody who knows."

Mr. McKinney interrupted with a wave of his hand. "Now, T.J., builders sound like cool people but I'm sure that they have some weaknesses, right?"

T.J. smiled as he nodded his head. He was overly familiar with the weaknesses of one builder, himself. "Because builders are looking at all of the details, they often focus on the reasons things can't be done. And they love to 'do it themselves,' so sometimes they struggle to align themselves with the ideas of a visionary…even though they know that they have to work together to be successful."

T.J. stopped to take a breath and Mr. McKinney jumped in. "So, as a builder, how do you feel about visionaries?"

T.J. thought for a second before responding. How did he feel about Andy? "I admire them and I want to put our skill sets together so we can accomplish the goal," T.J. said firmly.

Amber dropped by the table. "Here's a refill," she said, as T.J. took one of his last two bites of biscuit. "You fellas need anything else today?"

Mr. McKinney smiled as he replied. "No thanks, I think we're almost done."

"Well, no hurry to leave, but here's the check. You can pay John at the front."

Mr. McKinney looked at his watch. "Well, T.J., I've got a few more minutes before I need to head over to the store and there's one type we haven't discussed. If you want anything to be successful in the long term, you need maintainers to keep it going. From what I've seen, they are the most misunderstood of the three types. Let me tell you a story about how critical they are.

"In Jerusalem, around the year 1000 BC, a guy known as King David reigns over the kingdoms of Israel and Judah. For David's people, the Ark of the Covenant (a wooden box covered in gold) represents God's presence on Earth. For hundreds of years, the Ark had lived in a tent made of camel hair. Now, David says to the prophet Nathan, 'You know, I have a pretty nice house here but we have the presence of God living in a tent…maybe we should fix that.' A great idea says Nathan, but the next day, Nathan comes back to tell David, 'You know, that temple thing we talked about yesterday is a great idea, but your son will build it, not you.' Now, David could have gotten huffy with God, or even Nathan. I can almost hear him now: 'You know, God, this is a really good idea…I can see your temple now, huge columns, gold-plated walls, a great place for a great God.' But David didn't do that. Nope, he spends his life drawing up the plans, making alliances to ensure that all of the supplies are ready, and, we assume, spending time with his son, Solomon, to describe the plan.

"David dies, and Solomon becomes king. Solomon could have taken all of the supplies that David collected for the temple and created a stadium or an even bigger palace, but he doesn't. He asks his father's allies for help and, using the vision that David passed on to him, builds the temple. Seven years of work and it's done—only seven years. David's preparation paid off, but only after he died. I have to assume that David had a front-row seat, watching the temple dedication ceremonies with a smile on his face."

"So wait a minute," interrupted T.J. "David had a vision, prepared for it to be realized, and never saw it come to pass? That seems like cruel and unusual punishment!"

Mr. McKinney replied, "Well, T.J., I've seen that most of the organizations, initiatives, and ideas that last a long time have a handoff plan in place. I think King David knew that he turned his vision over to Solomon. Now, listen to what happened next.

"The temple is built and there's a big party. If this had happened today, the temple would have fallen into disrepair within a couple of decades, right? Not this place of worship. The Levites, one of the twelve tribes of Israel, have the job of maintaining the temple and that's just what they do. They clean the temple, make the daily sacrifices, and celebrate the festivals...all those regular activities that must be done to keep the nation in the right relationship with God. The Levites remained faithful to their responsibilities for over four hundred years until the temple was destroyed."

T.J. realized that the only time he had moved during the entire story was to comment on the unfairness of the concept. Blinking his eyes, he moved his mouth but words didn't come easily. He was so taken by the concept that maintainers were necessary for long-term success that he wasn't at all ready for what came next. Mr. McKinney looked him straight in the eye. "So, T.J., what's bugging you? Is it a maintainer that can't see the big picture, a builder who doesn't delegate anything to you because he's doing it all, or a visionary that never has any concrete ideas and just talks in generalities? Since builders and visionaries usually co-exist pretty well, I'm guessing your boss is a maintainer and you're struggling to understand why he wants you to focus on things you think are pretty minor details."

T.J. looked down at his plate. There was one bite left. If he took it, he could buy himself a few seconds to think while he chewed. He filled his fork, placed it in his mouth, and chewed very slowly. He was stunned that this old grandfatherly guy had been able to describe his problems so succinctly—and with almost no knowledge of the situation! He finished chewing and took a drink. "This kind of sounds silly talking to a guy who owns a hardware store but, you hit the nail on the head. My new boss is focused on stuff I think is completely inconsequential. It's all necessary to keep this ship afloat, but I'd really like to be figuring out how to build a new ship! My old boss was always coming up with big ideas and he counted on me to implement them. I miss that," T.J. said, almost whispering.

"Well, looks like it's time for me to go open the store," said Mr. McKinney as he pushed his chair back from the table. "You're a smart guy, T.J. You're going to figure this thing out. Why don't you think about it this weekend? I'll bet you will have a plan built and ready to go on Monday morning." And with that, Mr. McKinney stood up, placed his hand on T.J.'s shoulder, and made his way to the door.

T.J. sat at the table for a couple more minutes, organizing the thoughts in his head. When he decided to get up from the table, he realized that Mr. McKinney had taken the bill for breakfast with him. T.J. stopped at the register. "I was eating breakfast with Reid McKinney over there in the corner. I need to pay my part of the bill."

The gentleman behind the cash register laughed. "Reid McKinney's been eatin' here for over twenty years. I ain't never known him to let a guest pay for a meal. He took care of the bill and left a good tip for Amber, too. Now you get on out of here and get ready for that little one. He'll be here before you know it!" T.J. smiled, as he thought, *No secrets in this town.*

"Yes, sir. Thank you!" He opened the door into a day that seemed a little sunnier than he had seen in a while.

# Epilogue

On Sunday afternoon, while Jill took a well-deserved nap, T.J. sat down in the living room and pulled out a pad of paper. He began to write out a plan for implementing the new scorecard for his shop. First, he recreated the boards that he had painted on the walls in the baby's room:

| Weekly | |
|---|---|
| **Results (# per day)** | **Actions** |
| **Plan Achieved (%)** | **Actions** |

| Monthly | |
|---|---|
| Production | Plan |
| Yearly | |
| Production | Plan |

With Andy, he could have looked forward to a good discussion on Monday about the topic. However, he was pretty sure it wouldn't go that way with Hoyt. Since Hoyt visited Jill in the hospital, T.J. had found he had a lot more patience when dealing with him. He wondered, *How can I explain this idea so Hoyt understands its importance to me?* He was pretty sure that Hoyt would react more positively to the finished product than one that was in progress. In fact, maybe that was one reason Hoyt had gotten promoted to this job. His previous position in the maintenance area was focused on keeping the status quo. In production, if you kept the status quo, you went out of business pretty quickly. T.J. would have to bring a well thought out idea and a few success stories to show Hoyt the idea was ready to implement.

To implement the new indicators, he already had Eric on board but he would definitely need a few weeks in order to have the results for those success stories. He decided to keep the idea under wraps for two weeks. He wrote that on the sheet of paper under the board designs. Adapting his style to Hoyt's was going to be a challenge. He would have to provide more detail than he thought was necessary and find others around him to help test his ideas. T.J. took a deep breath. Finding a new way of working with Hoyt was going to be difficult but he now saw the way forward.

He heard the floorboards squeak in the hallway just before Jill came into view. "I had a pretty good nap until junior decided it was time to kick me in the kidneys or spine or something. He's going to be here soon. Got any ideas on names?"

T.J. put his notes down on the coffee table. "Well, kinda," he said slowly. "How about Reid?"

# So, now what?

After many years of observing people in the business and civic arenas, I noticed a pattern that gave me insight into why people acted the way they did in many situations. I found that it applied at work, at home, and in volunteer organizations. It even applies across international borders. I am not a psychologist, nor have I done any academic research in this area. However, I believe that knowing what type you are can make a big difference in how you see yourself...and knowing what type others are can help you (and whatever it is you are involved in) be more successful. That's why I've tried to bring the concept of visionaries, builders, and maintainers to life for you with the preceding story.

At the end of his breakfast with T.J., Reid McKinney described three types of people that were required to construct and take care of the temple. David was the visionary. He had an idea and he spent his life focused on that idea and how to make it reality.[1] That didn't occur until he passed the baton to Solomon, the builder. Solomon took someone else's idea and made it a reality using the skills God had given him.[2] When the temple was built, someone had to take care of it. That task fell to the Levites, who were the maintainers. They thrived on the regularity of this service and for almost four hundred years, some member of that family took care of God's 'house' on Earth.[3] [5]

I would be hard pressed to list more than four or five ideas/organizations around today that existed in 1600, and I am guessing that you would have a similar problem. Why is it that some ideas succeed for a short time and then don't last? Sometimes, it seems that even better ideas don't take root! I think that the secret to success is in the people making it happen. There is a place for everyone; this book will help you see everyone is in his/her place. In this section, I hope to help you understand: 1) each of the types a little better and 2) how powerful a force these three types of people can be when they operate within their strengths and with each other. At the end of this section, I believe you'll see people and their interactions with things, projects, and each other in a new and powerful way.

Before we talk about each of the types in detail, let's take a quiz. Which of the three profiles below seems most like you?

A) You are a teacher and have been for the past ten years. The most rewarding part of your job is watching the children leave at the end of the school year, ready for the next grade.

B) You are a dentist and truly enjoy your job. Although you have to admit that mouths look pretty similar, you enjoy ensuring your patients will have their teeth for years to come.

C) You are a stay at home parent. You enjoy finding projects to do with your children and have a good time working together with them to complete the activity. However, while you are working on it, you are already thinking about the next big thing to do together.

**Profile A** is typical of *builders*. Builders like to 'construct' things (people, organizations, processes, relationships) until they no longer see opportunities for improvement. Then, it's time to find something else to build.

**Profile B** is typical of *maintainers*. People who match this profile typically like being 'experts.' They excel at doing the same thing, the same way every time.

**Profile C** is typical of *visionaries*. They seldom live in the present, preferring to look at the opportunities of the future. They are big idea people, often seeing opportunities before anyone else.

In the following pages, we'll explore all three of these profiles. As you read about them, look for clues about yourself but also, clues about others around you—your spouse, children, colleagues, boss, employees, etc.

# Visionaries

As a child, I was fascinated by outer space and the brave men and women who traveled there. From Sputnik to John Glenn to Christa McAuliffe, I was a space junkie. In the United States, NASA was the organization behind the ability of Neil Armstrong to collect moon rocks or Sally Ride to do weightless cartwheels. Clearly, NASA has experienced its share of ups (moonwalks, international space station) and downs (the Apollo 1, Challenger, and Columbia disasters) but it continues to improve life on Earth by reaching for the heavens.

Let's look at NASA's Apollo program of the 1960s and '70s. The moon was an enticing piece of space real estate. Could the United States send someone there...and bring them back? To use a phrase from Jim Collins's book, *Good to Great*, it was clearly a "Big, Hairy, Audacious, Goal (BHAG)." But could it be achieved? On May 25, 1961, President John F. Kennedy announced his support for the Apollo program as part of a special address to a joint session of Congress:

*First, I believe that this nation should commit itself to achieving the goal, before this decade is out, of landing a man on the Moon and returning him safely to the Earth. No single space project in this period will be more impressive to mankind, or more important in the long-range exploration of space; and none will be so difficult or expensive to accomplish.* [1]

Were you aware that when Kennedy made this speech, only one American had ever been into space? Regardless of the current situation, Kennedy made his fellow citizens believe that something that seemed impossible...was possible. That's a key trait of a visionary—the seeming ability to see into the future. There are many famous examples of visionaries. For example, Winston Churchill predicted at age seventeen that he would save England—forty-nine years before the start of World War Two![2] It was said of Dale Earnhardt, the Hall of Fame NASCAR driver, that he "could see two, three years down the road when we couldn't hardly see two, three weeks down the road."[3] His son, Dale Earnhardt, Jr., seems to have inherited that gene as well. His JR Motorsports team is one of the most powerful in the second tier Nationwide Series.

The people above are just a few of the examples of visionaries that we can find in the worlds of business, politics, education, sports, and more. Visionaries typically have great charisma and people who 'buy in' to their visions will do almost anything for them. The vision that they have can come from inside them (ideas, dreams, etc.) while others are 'birthed' as we see opportunities around us. Ideas may come to visionaries at any time. In fact, I know a successful visionary who keeps a pad of paper beside his bed so he doesn't 'lose' any of the ideas that might come to him during the night.

Another interesting trait of visionaries is that they don't see many (if any) reasons why things can't be done. Once they have a vision, they can believe so strongly in it that they are not easily dissuaded regardless of the information surrounding them. For example, Darwin Smith, CEO of Kimberly-Clark, saw that the consumer paper-products industry was the wave of the future for his company. He was so convinced that he sold the paper mills on which the company had been built for twenty years in order to invest in today's everyday brands like Huggies and Kleenex. He was criticized by the business media, and Wall Street analysts even downgraded the stock.[4]

After reading the descriptions above, you might think that being a visionary sounds like a pretty cool gig.

Step 1: Go for a retreat in the woods

Step 2: Get some ideas

Step 3: Come back and start impressing people with my amazing eyes into the future

Not so fast…visionaries have their own special set of challenges.

First, they must travel light. That doesn't mean that they only get to use carry-on luggage when traveling. No, because the role of a visionary is to get the ball rolling, they might not get to see all of their ideas implemented. Once a vision has been passed on to the right people, the visionary may need to move on so that they can do something else. In fact, visionaries who stay too long in one place can actually impede the implementation of their vision.

Also, as a visionary, you see things as they will be in the future that no one else can see with their 'eyes of today.' That means that people may scoff at your ideas. Powered flight, space travel, deep sea diving, accessing your e-mail in the palm of your hand—all of these things were fiction until someone had a vision and made fiction fact.

Finally, as a visionary, the human race expects that you will use your vision for the good of others. We all really want your vision to make a difference for humanity. Unfortunately, not all visionaries (examples: Jim Jones, Adolf Hitler) translate their vision into positive actions for the rest of the world. So, first do no harm. But, visionaries must *do* something! There's a clear difference between a dreamer and a visionary. A visionary takes responsibility for passing the vision along to construct a better future. Dreamers are visionary people who are guilty of not sharing their ideas. But wait, you say, I'm a visionary but I don't know who to share my vision with! Read on, my friend, read on.

# Builders

V isitors to the city of Barcelona, the second largest city in Spain, are confronted with some questions even as they begin to plan their visit. Such questions as:

"Who is responsible for that tiled salamander in the Parc Guell?"

"Was the cathedral Sagrada Familia inspired by a sandcastle?"

"Who dreamed up these buildings with rooflines made of whimsical curves and façades that are a combination of such fantastic colors and shapes?"

All three of these fantastic creations (and more) are the work of Antoni Gaudi, whose life's work led to him earning the nickname "God's Architect."[1] You might think that someone whose creations are so fantastic and creative would be an example of a visionary. You might also guess, based on the title of this chapter, that I believe Gaudi to be an excellent example of a builder. The 'vision' that Gaudi was trying to build was a combination of the natural creations he saw around him. As a builder, Gaudi's responsibility was to the completion of the vision that was passed on to him. He took this very seriously, even spending the last eleven years of his life living in the basement of the Sagrada Familia (begun in 1882 with a target completion date of 2026 [one hundred years after Gaudi's death]).[2] Gaudi shows us that, regardless of where vision comes from, builders are needed to take a vision and make it reality.

In the previous chapter, we discussed John F. Kennedy's vision to land a man on the moon. Clearly, that's not a commitment most of us would make without something to back it up. Kennedy had Werner von Braun, builder extraordinaire, who had been working on rockets for over thirty years and specifically the Saturn rocket, which carried the United States' precious human payload into orbit in 1969, for at least three years.[3] Von Braun continued to build the United States' presence in space into the 1970s as the first director of the Marshall Space Flight Center.[4]

We've also previously discussed the Earnhardt family from the world of American motorsports. If father and son are recognized as visionaries today, it's because they had builders to translate that vision into something lasting. Coincidentally, for both Earnhardt Senior and Junior, a woman close to them was able to understand and implement the vision. Teresa Earnhardt, Dale Sr.'s wife, built the multi-million-dollar racing team Dale Earnhardt Inc. based on his vision. Similarly, Dale Jr.'s sister, Kelley Earnhardt Elledge, built JR motorsports. It's been said of Dale Jr.'s vision that Elledge "takes all of that and puts it on paper and makes it be operational, makes it successful."[5]

That's not to say that visionary to builder is a 'one-to-one' relationship. Let's take the example of Franklin Delano Roosevelt. As he accepted the Democratic nomination for president of the United States in 1932, he promised the following:

*Throughout the nation men and women, forgotten in the political philosophy of the Government, look to us here for guidance and for more equitable opportunity to share in the distribution of national wealth... I pledge myself to a new deal for the American people. This is more than a political campaign. It is a call to arms.*[6]

Roosevelt had a vision of what the government could do to help Americans recover from the Great Depression. However, he couldn't put that vision in place all by himself. That's why he surrounded himself with a group of advisors called the "Brain Trust." This group of men and one woman helped him construct the vision of a 'New Deal.'[7]

So, let's talk about some of the specifics of being a builder. Notice that the examples we've discussed have built cathedrals (Gaudi), companies (the Earnhardts), and, among other things, the Civilian Conservation Corps (the Brain Trust). So it's clear that builders build 'things.' However, they also build relationships. Builders might not know the answer, but they usually know somebody who knows. Therefore, they usually have an excellent network of people that help them by providing the right expertise at the right time.

Because they are looking at all of the details, builders often see all of the reasons why something *can't* be done. This puts them in natural opposition with the visionaries who, as a reminder, usually see only the reasons things *can* be done. Therefore, finding a good visionary-builder pairing can be difficult. A good builder must remain 'realistically faithful' to the vision. They have to implement the vision while respecting the realities of budgets, resource constraints, and people who just plain think this is a bad idea. If they aren't careful, builders can find themselves struck between a visionary who feels like their vision has been compromised and a lot of impacted people who don't think it has been compromised enough!

Remember in the last chapter we talked about the need for visionaries to 'travel light' and be ready to move once their vision is passed on to the right people. Because builders need physical tools (pen, paper, computer, tablet) and virtual ones (networks, previous accomplishments), they typically don't move as quickly or voluntarily. If a builder has a vision to implement, their focus and drive can keep them focused on one 'project' for years or even decades!

So, if the visionary introduces the idea and the builder implements it we're done, right? Not exactly. Think about your home or apartment. It was most likely built in a period of months or, at most, years.

If you don't take the time to fix the small problems (leaks, landscaping, etc.), they become big ones. In fact, I recently saw a subdivision that was only partially built and never inhabited. In just a few years, those structures will be completely worthless! So, who can help you take that bright, shiny vision that you just translated into reality and make it endure? Maintainers.

# Maintainers

**E**very month, over ten billion pages on Wikipedia are viewed around the world. Who is responsible for the over twenty-two million articles in 285 languages? It could be that nice, elderly gentleman down the street, the babysitter next door who drives a car covered in smiley faces, or the summer intern in the Finance department. In short, it could be anyone—and that's just the way Wikipedia co-founder Jimmy Wales envisioned it. Wales's vision carried the company for six years. In fact, from 2001 to 2007, Wikipedia grew from one article to over two million, and from the outside, it looked like a dot com success story.[1]

On the inside, things looked different. The non-profit Wikimedia Foundation had a staff of seven housed in a Florida strip-mall and it was looking for an executive director after the initial one had left after eight months. On April 16, after visiting the Wikipedia Talk page about the shootings at Virginia Tech in Blacksburg, Virginia, an unemployed thirty-nine-year-old in Canada happened on the Foundation's opening for a director. Sue Gardner applied and put in place an organization that could better meet the needs of the millions of Wikipedia contributors.[2]

If we translate the Wikipedia story into terms from this book, Wales was clearly the visionary. His ideas got the company to the point where a builder was needed and Gardner has successfully filled that role. How does Wikipedia continue to be relevant ten years after its founding when many other (better-funded) sites have failed? I believe the answer is the maintainers. Wikipedia has a base of millions of 'average citizens' that police themselves and ensure that the content of Wikipedia meets guidelines that they establish. This model requires little long-term investment (recent yearly fundraising campaigns had a goal of fifteen to twenty million dollars) yet guarantees time-liness. Wikipedia contributors are known to 'race' for the honor of updating a page after a newsworthy event (sports championships, disasters, new restaurant locations, etc.). Wikipedia shows us that the combination of a visionary, builder, and maintainer has the ability to create a successful long-term business model.

We all do some maintainer roles in our life. Cutting the grass? You're maintaining it so it doesn't get over a certain height. Cleaning the bathroom? You're making sure that the toilet or shower, or sink looks as good as it did when it was new. Changing oil in the car (or paying someone else to)? Regular oil changes keep your engine running smoothly delivering better performance now and hopefully, better resale value later. However, the necessity of maintaining doesn't mean everyone enjoys it. The guy who mows his yard several times per week to keep his grass exactly one inch high does it because he enjoys it. Me? I mow my yard every week or two to keep my grass less than five or six inches high. So, the first step in identifying a maintainer is to find someone who enjoys keeping some things looking (or running) just the way they did before.

Once on board, maintainers are great rule followers and are especially gifted at sticking to the plan. They excel in doing the step-by-step activities that Visionaries and Builders absolutely hate. Typically, maintainers aren't 'think outside the box' kind of people and they're more than happy with that. That's why a maintainer that's 'on board' with the vision and how it's built is worth his or her weight in gold. Since maintainers aren't usually creating change, they can be less comfortable with it than visionaries and builders. Maintainers are most comfortable when they can see a finished product before being asked to make a transition. They can keep the ship afloat while the visionary is coming up with the next big thing and the builder is covered in the dust of changing things to match the vision.

One surprising thing about maintainers is that they get little respect. The world is fascinated with those who envision and create amazing things. Thomas Edison and his more than one thousand patents, Michelangelo's frescoes on the ceiling of the Sistine Chapel, Ludwig van Beethoven and his symphonies—they are all famous because of their amazing contributions to society. Yet, without maintainers who use the ideas of Edison or ensure the daily care of the Sistine Chapel or continue to perform Beethoven's works, we would lose their ideas to the sands of time. Someone must keep great ideas in front of us. Maintainers do it joyfully with little recognition.

Finally, maintainers are excellent at long-term commitment. Twenty-five years with the same company, in the same building, doing roughly the same job? That's a formula that would drive most visionaries and builders insane, yet maintainers like this are the backbone of most global organizations (both for-profit and not-for-profit) in the world today. They are clearly the backbone of Wikipedia. It's incredible to think that seven people in the world, regardless of their intelligence and capacity to work, could produce a comprehensive encyclopedia of human knowledge in nearly three hundred languages. Yet it was done. Not by just seven lonely souls, but by millions who are dedicated to respecting Jimmy Wales's vision of "an open source, collaborative encyclopedia, open to contribution by ordinary people."[3]

# Conclusion

When your type and role at home, work, or elsewhere match, you're likely to be extremely productive and happy with what you're doing. But what happens when, as a young visionary, your ideas are ignored while you must build the dreams of others? Or, as a builder, you're expected to maintain the thirty-six-step process that you just created. Or, as a maintainer, you're in a role where everyone looks to you to provide strategy and direction for the future? When your visionary, builder, or maintainer tendencies don't match up with your role in an organization, there's a high likelihood of frustration and burnout. Today, I challenge you to begin looking for roles that play to your strengths. Then, look around you to see what types you need to surround yourself with. None of the three types can productively exist in a vacuum. In fact, the types are multiplicative, not additive. It's not Visionary + Builder + Maintainer; it's Visionary x Builder x Maintainer—each type's strengths multiply the others.

**A visionary imagines, a builder implements, and a maintainer improves performance.**

You've read the book, now take the assessment!

Visit **kennethefields.com** and click on the Assessment link for a free download. This tool can help you identify both your change management personality type and the types of those around you.

# Appendix 1

short summary of some characteristics of the three types of people.

**<u>Visionaries</u>**

*<u>Time</u>* – Focused on tomorrow – "What should it look like?"

*<u>Strengths</u>* – Seeing the big picture and being an "idea person."

*<u>Weaknesses</u>* – Implementation of their ideas; specifically, unrealistic estimation of resources.

*<u>Opinion concerning change</u>* – "I love it! I can't imagine leaving things the way they are."

*<u>Examples</u>* – John F. Kennedy, Jimmy Wales

## Builders

*Time* – Focused on today – "What do I need to do to get us where we need to go?"

*Strengths* – Planning, organizing

*Weaknesses* – Out of the box thinking, creativity.

*Opinion concerning change* – "It's OK if I'm the one responsible for it."

*Examples* – Werner von Braun, Sue Gardener

## Maintainers

*Time* – Focused on yesterday –"How can I get this mess to look the way it did before—'the right way?'"

*Strengths* – Consistency, Dependability

*Weaknesses* – Seeing the big picture, embracing change.

*Opinion concerning change* – "No, thank you."

*Examples* – Since their contributions are often 'behind the scenes,' well-known examples are hard to find. Wikipedia editors are en example of maintainers.

# Notes

**So, now what?**

1    New International Version, 2 Samuel 7

2    1 Kings 5–6

3    1 Chronicles 23

4    "Siege of Jerusalem (70)," Wikipedia, http://en.wikipedia.org/wiki/Siege_of_Jerusalem_(70), retrieved July 29, 2012.

**Visionaries**

1    "John F. Kennedy," Wikipedia, http://en.wikipedia.org/wiki/John_F._Kennedy, retrieved October 9, 2012.

[2]     Richard Langworth, Editor, *Churchill By Himself: The Definitive Collection of Quotations* (New York: PublicAffairs, 2008), 497.

[3]     Fleischman, B. (2001, June 1). Norris carries on Earnhardt's vision. *Lewiston Sun Journal*, p. C2. Retrieved from http://news.google.com/newspapers?nid=1914&dat=20010601&id=YtRKAAAAIBAJ&sjid=lvMMAAAAIBAJ&pg=4702,97900.

[4]     Jim Collins, *Good to Great* (New York: Collins, 2001), 18–20.


## Builders

[1]     "Antoni Gaudí," Wikipedia, http://en.wikipedia.org/wiki/Antoni_Gaud%C3%AD, retrieved July 29, 2012.

[2]     "Sagrada Família," Wikipedia, http://en.wikipedia.org/wiki/Sagrada_Fam%C3%ADlia, retrieved July 29, 2012.

[3]     "Saturn (rocket family)," Wikipedia, http://en.wikipedia.org/wiki/Saturn_(rocket_family), retrieved July 29, 2012.

[4]     "Wernher von Braun," Wikipedia, http://en.wikipedia.org/wiki/Wernher_von_Braun, retrieved July 29, 2012.

[5]     Newton, D. (2007, 12 April). Earnhardt Jr. on fast track in business world, too. ESPN.com, retrieved

from http://sports.espn.go.com/rpm/columns/story?
seriesId=2&columnist=newton_david&id=2833053.

6 "New Deal", Wikipedia, http://en.wikipedia.org/
wiki/New_deal, retrieved May 18, 2008.

7 "Brain Trust", Wikipedia, http://en.wikipedia.
org/wiki/Brain_trust, retrieved May 18, 2008.

## Maintainers

1 "History of Wikipedia," Wikipedia, http://
en.wikipedia.org/wiki/History_of_Wikipedia,
retrieved July 25, 2012.

2 Valby, K (2011, April), "Librarian to the World,"
*Fast Company*, *154*, http://www.fastcompany.com/
magazine/154/librarian-to-the-world.html, retrieved
July 30, 2012.

3 "History of Wikipedia," Wikipedia.

Made in the USA
Lexington, KY
15 June 2013